SIMPLY
DAIRY FREE

D1076109

C334020376

SIMPLY
DAIRY FREE

FRESH & SIMPLE LACTOSE-FREE RECIPES FOR HEALTHY EATING EVERY DAY

LESLEY WATERS

hamlyn

Contents

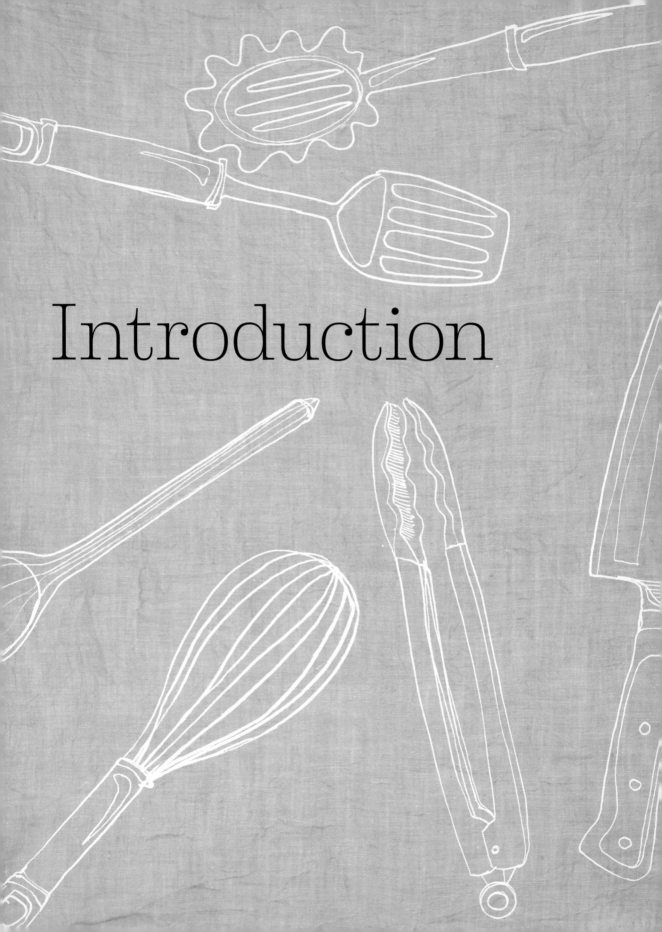

Introduction

Millions of people are affected by lactose intolerance, and many others these days simply prefer to avoid dairy products. When we first opened the doors of our cookery school in Dorset ten years ago, we would receive the occasional request for dairy- or gluten-free options, but as time has gone by, we have seen major changes in what our students want: the courses offering healthier choices and those catering for more specialized dietary needs are growing in popularity. More and more people are waking up to the fact that healthy eating is not about 'diet foods' but a really positive way of taking care of yourself and your family. *Simply Dairy Free* proposes a modern, lighter and cleaner way of eating – a way of combining great ingredients with a simple, dairy-free approach.

I have always been interested in healthy eating, but I first got involved in dairy-free cooking when my mum was diagnosed with colitis years ago and needed to change her diet as a result. Back then, it was still difficult to find products that could be used in place of milk, cream or cheese, but this has changed, with major supermarkets and health food shops now all stocking a good range of tasty alternatives. *Simply Dairy Free* will show you how to have fun and success in the kitchen without feeling that you are missing out.

We start off with a range of recipes that are perfect for breakfast and brunch, some of which also make quick snacks or starters ... real fast food, but fresh! The 'Big Salads & Super Soups' in chapter 2 are meals in themselves: simple and satisfying, they really hit the spot. 'Weekday Favourites' features speedy and delicious home-cooked suppers for family and friends: you'll find here cheats and swaps for all those favourite dishes you think are off limits, like Mac & Cheese, Spaghetti Carbonara, Creamy Chicken Curry, Pizza and Classic Quiche. 'Weekend Delights' covers spreads designed to impress your guests: you'll find starters, main courses and special weekend food to be enjoyed indoors or alfresco. Proving that you can have your cake and eat it, 'The Clean Bake' covers scrumptious cookies, pastries and breads, while 'Puddings & Sweeties' offers a selection of dairy-free desserts, including Raspberry & Banana Instant Ice Cream, Mega Saucy Chocolate Pud & Homemade Custard Sauce. Finally, 'Basics' brings together a few staples of the dairy-free kitchen, from Cashew Honey Cream and DIY Fresh Almond Milk to a variety of stocks, sauces and dressings that will add kick and a real edge to your dishes.

So, whether you suffer from lactose intolerance or you would simply prefer to ditch the dairy, this book will show you how easy it can be to transform the way you cook and eat by making only a few small changes. While writing, testing and cooking the recipes in *Simply Dairy Free*, I realized that the dairy-free way of life is not about missing out – it's quite the opposite. This book is all about great-tasting, mouth-watering food for all occasions that everyone can enjoy!

Recipe Finder

Breakfast & Brunch

	Page	Contains no eggs	Contains no nuts	Gluten/wheat-free	Vegetarian	Vegan
Banana & Peanut Butter Smoothie	12	•		•	•	•
Strawberry & Vanilla Cream Shake	12	•	•	•	•	•
Cinnamon & Vanilla French Toasts	15				•	
Banana & Coconut Popover Pancakes with Maple & Lime	16		•		•	
Scrambled Eggs with Pesto Toasts	19		•		•	
Chillied Eggs on Onion Rice	20		•		•	
Brunch Bread & Chorizo Omelette	22		•			
Hot Chilli Baked Tomatoes	22	•	•		•	•
Pan Bagne	23	•	•		•	•
Beetroot Vodka Shots	25	•	•	•	•	•
Breakfast Bacon Popcorn	25	•	•	•		
Mexican Corn Cakes with Avocado Crush	26		•	•	•	•
Spiked Balsamic Beef Tomatoes	29		•			

Big Salads & Super Soups

	Page	Contains no eggs	Contains no nuts	Gluten/wheat-free	Vegetarian	Vegan
Tuscan Bread & Tomato Salad with Sweet Peppers & Black Olives	32	•	•		•	•
Broccoli Coleslaw	34	•	•	•	•	•
Asparagus with Tomato & Pea Dressing	34	•	•	•	•	•
Bacon & Croute Salad with Chilli & Leek Poached Egg	35		•			
Chunky Chip Salad with Ham Hock & Puy Lentil Dressing	37	•	•	•		
Noodle Salad with Crispy Duck Legs	38		•			
Pineapple & Smoked Chicken Sambal	41	•	•			
Niçoise Rustic Board	42	•	•	•		
Purple Sprouting Broccoli Soup with Tapenade Croutes	45	•	•		•	•
Parsnip & Chilli Soup with Cardamom Crumbs	46	•	•			
Thai Broth with Crispy Noodles	47	•	•	•	•	•
Spiced Sweet Potato Chowder	48	•	•	•	•	•
Barley Minestrone	51	•	•		•	•
Creamy Corn & Haddock Chowder	52	•	•	•		
Pea & Bacon Chowder	55	•	•	•		
Skillet Scones	55				•	•

Weekday Favourites

	Page	Contains no eggs	Contains no nuts	Gluten/wheat-free	Vegetarian	Vegan
Pan-fried Vegetable Bhaji with Eggs & Wilted Greens	58		•	•	•	
White Bean Creamy Hummus with Broad Bean Salad & Dukkah	60	•			•	•
Basil & Bean Linguine with Crispy Crumbs	61	•	•		•	
Altogether Pasta Pronto	63	•	•		•	
Double-baked Mac & Cheese with Roasted Vine Tomatoes	64	•	•		•	
Summer Fresh Pea & Sunblush Risotto	67	•	•	•	•	
Mushroom Stroganoff with Walnuts & Rocket	68	•		•	•	•
Welsh Rarebit Melts	70	•	•		•	
Pasta Paella with Basil Ink	71	•	•			
Fish Cachets	72	•	•			
Creamy Garlic Mash	73	•	•	•	•	•
Creamy Lemon Potatoes with Herby Salmon	75	•		•		
Fiery Fish Pie	76	•	•			
Cracked Coriander Griddled Mackerel Fillets with Lentils	77	•	•	•		
Garlic & Thyme Chicken with Cannellini & Potato Mash	78	•	•	•		
Chorizo-crusted Chicken with Apple & Sage Cassoulet	81	•	•			
Smoky Quesadilla Melts with Chicken, Coriander & Avocado	82		•			
Sesame Chicken Lickin'	85		•			
Creamy Chicken Curry	86	•	•			
Spaghetti alla Carbonara	89		•			
Pizza Pizza Pizza	90	•	•			
Classic Quiche	93		•		•	
Roasted Cauliflower & Broccoli Mornay with a Chorizo Crumb	94	•	•		•	
Luxury Beef & Prosciutto Lasagne with a Cheesy Nutmeg Sauce	97	•	•			
Boston Bean Bake Topped with Olive Oil & Herb Dumplings	98	•	•			
Soft Beef Kofta Meatballs in Sticky Glaze	101		•			
Nutty Noodles with Wilted Greens & Sticky Beef	102					
Pork & Prune Medallions with Creamy Cider & Mustard Sauce	103	•	•	•		

Weekend Delights

	Page	Contains no eggs	Contains no nuts	Gluten/wheat-free	Vegetarian	Vegan
Melon, Ham & Pine Nut Salad	106	•	•	•		•
Asparagus with Watercress & Candied Walnut Salad	109	•	•	•	•	•
Vintage Egg Mayo with Tapenade & Cress	110		•	•		
Smoked Trout Bruschetta with Orange & Dill Relish	113	•	•	•		
Hot-smoked Salmon Horseradish Crème with Fresh Spinach Sauce	114	•		•		
Roasted Salt & Pepper Pears & Serrano Platter	117	•	•	•		
Duck with Warm Pomegranate, Puy Lentil & Orange Salad	118	•	•	•		
Potato & Celeriac Pie with Rapeseed Crust	121		•	•	•	•
Crab & Ginger Tart with Soy chilli Dressing	122		•	•		
Chicken Tagine with Red Lentils & Rice	125	•	•	•		
Saffron-baked Orange Poussin with Crispy-topped Risotto	126	•	•	•		
Roasted Guinea Fowl with Cardamom Bread Sauce	127	•				
Slow-cooked Lamb with Lemon & Oregano	128	•	•	•		
Salt & Thyme Crusted Pork Belly	130	•	•	•		
Rich Steak & Venison Pie with a Black Pepper Crust	131	•	•	•	•	•
Hot Black Bean Sweet Chunky Chilli with Steak Burgers & Skinny Chips	133	•	•	•	•	•

The Clean Bake

	Page	Contains no eggs	Contains no nuts	Gluten/wheat-free	Vegetarian	Vegan
Caramelized Onion & Spelt Flatbread	137	•	•		•	
Focaccia with Rosemary	138	•	•		•	•
Thyme, Garlic & Chilli Socca	139	•	•		•	•
Cracked Black Pepper & Figgy Bread	140	•	•		•	•
Bacon & Sage Cornbread	142	•				
Cheese & Chive Soda Bread	142	•				
Poppy Seed Grissini	143	•	•			
Vanilla Bean & Olive Oil Sandwich Cake	145		•		•	
Carrot & Walnut Muffelettas	146				•	
Lime Chocolate Cupcakes with Chilli Fondant Sauce	147				•	
Cinnamon & Orange Cookies	148	•	•		•	•
Cocoa Crumble Cookies	148	•	•		•	•
Coconut & Lime Cake	150		•	•	•	

Puddings & Sweeties

	Page	Contains no eggs	Contains no nuts	Gluten/wheat-free	Vegetarian	Vegan
Salted Caramel Banana Toffee Tatin	154	•	•		•	•
Coconut Rice Pudding with Griddled Pineapple	156	•	•	•	•	•
Summer Pudding Jam	157	•	•	•	•	•
Rhubarb & Vanilla Jam	157	•	•	•	•	•
Roasted Vanilla Nectarines with Sweet Wine & Berry Sauce	159	•	•	•	•	•
Meringue Nougats	159		•	•	•	
Plummy Chocolate Mousse with Pistachios	160		•	•	•	
Rhubarb, Almond & Orange Pudding Cake	163		•	•	•	
Mega Saucy Chocolate Pud with Orange Coconut Cream	164	•	•	•	•	
Raspberry & Banana Instant Ice Cream	167	•	•	•	•	
Cider Baked Apple Pie with Polenta Pastry	168		•	•	•	
Homemade Custard Sauce	169		•	•	•	
Frangipane Plum Tart	170		•	•	•	
Lemon Posset with Strawberries	171	•	•	•	•	
Sparkling Jellies	171	•	•	•	•	
Chocolate Polenta Cake with Espresso Syrup	172		•	•	•	
Chocolate & Apricot Fudgy Refrigerator Cake	175	•	•		•	•

Basics

	Page	Contains no eggs	Contains no nuts	Gluten/wheat-free	Vegetarian	Vegan
DIY Fresh Almond Milk	177	•		•	•	•
Cashew Honey Cream	178	•		•	•	
Instant Peanut Butter	178	•		•	•	•
Hazelnut Chocolate Spread	179	•		•	•	•
Cranberry, Red Cabbage & Juniper Jam	180	•	•	•	•	•
Roast Tomato Chutney	181	•	•	•	•	•
Sweet Pepper Chutney	181	•	•	•	•	•
Honey, Mustard & Cider Vinaigrette	182	•	•	•	•	
Warm Ginger & Orange Sesame Dressing	182	•	•	•	•	•
Soured Cream & Tarragon Dressing	183	•	•	•	•	
Smoked Pepper Rouille	183	•	•		•	
Classic Pesto	184	•	•		•	
Broad Bean & Basil Pistou	184	•	•		•	
Smoked Garlic & Chive Mayo	185		•	•	•	
Curry Gravy	185	•	•	•	•	
Citrus Chicken Stock Pot	186	•	•	•	•	
Bouquet Garni Stock	187	•	•	•	•	•

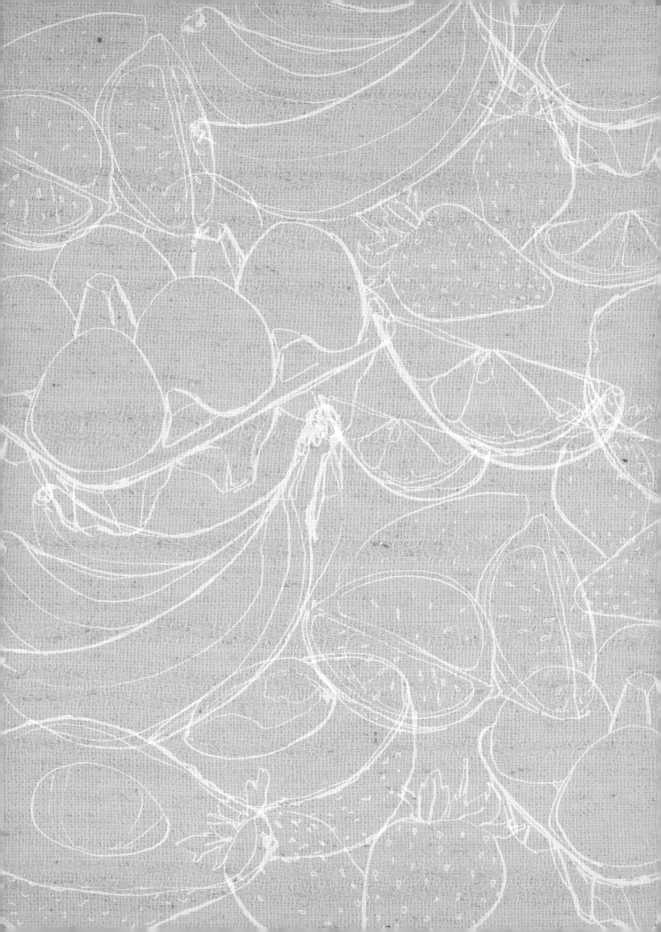

Breakfast
& Brunch

*My daughter Scout loves this Banana & Peanut Butter Smoothie...
rich, thick and creamy, like an American diner-style milkshake.
If you want it thinner, simply add a little more dairy-free milk
or ice cubes. The Strawberry & Vanilla Cream Shake (below) is
a classic combination of flavours. Make sure you use sweet, ripe
strawberries, but when not in season, frozen berries are a good
alternative. For an adult twist, I love to finish each glass with
a small grinding of black pepper. This is extra delicious
served with the Cocoa Crumble Cookies (see page 148).*

Banana & Peanut Butter Smoothie

MAKES 4 SMALL GLASSES
OR 2 LARGE GLASSES

2 small bananas

3 tablespoons Instant Peanut Butter
(see page 178)

6 ice cubes

300ml (½ pint) hazelnut, almond
(see page 177 for homemade)
or soya milk

Place everything in a blender and blend until really smooth.

Serve straight away.

Strawberry & Vanilla Cream Shake

MAKES 4 MEDIUM-SIZED GLASSES

300g (10oz) ripe strawberries, hulled

2 teaspoons vanilla bean paste

250ml (8fl oz) soya, oat or almond milk
(see page 177 for homemade)

50ml (2fl oz) dairy-free single cream

ice, to serve

Place all the ingredients in a blender and blend until creamy and smooth.

Half-fill 4 medium-sized glasses with ice and pour over the shake. Serve straight away.

A little bit of indulgence in the morning goes a long way – simply swap in some dairy-free milk for a delicious start to your day.

Cinnamon & Vanilla French Toasts with Bananas, Strawberries & Maple Syrup

SERVES 4

3 free-range eggs

300ml (½ pint) almond (see page 177 for homemade) or hazelnut milk

1 teaspoon ground cinnamon

1 teaspoon good-quality vanilla extract

rapeseed oil, for frying

½ dairy-free fruit or fig loaf, sliced into 8

sifted icing sugar, for dusting (optional)

2 bananas, cut into chunky slices

8 large strawberries, hulled and cut into quarters

maple syrup, to serve

Whisk together the eggs, milk, cinnamon and vanilla in a bowl.

Place a large, nonstick frying pan over a medium heat and add a splash of oil.

Dip the bread slices into the eggy mixture (not for too long or the bread will become soggy) and fry, in batches, for about 2 minutes each side or until golden brown and puffy. Remove from pan and keep warm in a low oven while you finish cooking all the toasts.

To serve, place 2 slices of French toast on each warmed serving plate and dust with icing sugar, if liked. Top with the bananas, strawberries and a good drizzle of maple syrup.

You can now buy fresh coconut milk from the chiller section in most supermarkets. However, you can use tinned coconut milk or even almond (see page 177 for a DIY version) or hazelnut milk if you prefer. Ring the changes by using sliced strawberries or peaches instead of bananas.

Banana & Coconut Popover Pancakes with Maple & Lime

SERVES 4

2 free-range eggs

30g (1oz) caster sugar

175g (6oz) plain flour

3 teaspoons baking powder

30g (1oz) unsweetened desiccated coconut, plus extra for sprinkling

275ml (9fl oz) coconut milk

sunflower oil, for frying

3 bananas, sliced

TO SERVE

maple syrup

lime wedges, for squeezing over

Beat together the eggs and sugar in a bowl. Mix in the flour, baking powder and desiccated coconut, then beat in the coconut milk until you have a smooth batter.

Heat a little oil in a large, nonstick frying pan. Ladle in the mixture – you will probably be able to cook the batter in batches of 2 or 3. Cook over a medium heat until small bubbles appear on the surface of the batter, then arrange slices of banana over the top of each and scatter with a little extra coconut. Cook for a further 1–2 minutes or until golden on the underside and firm enough to flip over.

Carefully flip the pancakes over and cook for a further 1–2 minutes or until just firm and golden. Flip on to a plate and keep warm in a low oven while you cook the remaining batter.

Serve piled up, drizzled with maple syrup and a squeeze of lime juice.

There is nothing more comforting than creamy scrambled eggs, and it's a real treat when combined with pesto and smothered on sourdough toasts. My favourite version is with the addition of smoked salmon or trout, whereas my husband likes his topped with very crispy bacon.

Scrambled Eggs with Pesto Toasts

SERVES 4

10 free-range eggs

2 tablespoons dairy-free single cream

4 large slices of dairy-free sourdough bread

1 tablespoon olive oil

5 tablespoons Classic Pesto (see page 184)

salt and pepper

Break the eggs into a bowl and use a fork to blend them, then gently beat in the cream and salt and pepper. Put the bread on to toast.

Pour the oil into a medium-sized, heavy-based nonstick saucepan and place over a medium heat. Add the egg mixture to the pan and, using a wooden spoon, start stirring briskly back and forth, getting into the corner of the pan and keeping the eggs moving all the time.

Once three-quarters of the egg is creamy and firm and the rest liquid, remove the pan from the heat. Keep on stirring but do not return to the heat – the eggs will cook in the residual heat of the pan.

To serve, spread the toast with a thick layer of the pesto. Top with the creamy scrambled eggs and serve straight away.

*I first had these steamed eggs with an Oriental twist in Thailand,
and they are a great hangover cure! It's now a family favourite,
not only for breakfast but for any time of day.*

Chillied Eggs on Onion Rice

SERVES 2

175g (6oz) basmati rice, washed

2 tablespoons rapeseed oil

1 bunch of spring onions, roughly chopped

2 large free-range eggs

2 tablespoons coriander leaves

1 red chilli, deseeded and cut into slivers

salt and pepper

Tabasco sauce or chilli ketchup, to serve

Cook the basmati rice according to the packet instructions, then drain well if necessary.

Heat 1 tablespoon of the oil in a nonstick frying pan, add the spring onions and fry for 3–4 minutes until golden and soft. Stir into the cooked rice, season to taste with salt and pepper and set to one side.

Heat the remaining oil in the frying pan and crack in the eggs.

Sprinkle the eggs with the coriander leaves and chilli, and season well with salt and pepper. Cover the pan with a tight-fitting lid and allow the eggs to gently steam until just cooked.

To serve, place a dome of onion rice in the centre of 2 large, warmed plates. Top each with an egg and shake over Tabasco or chilli ketchup.

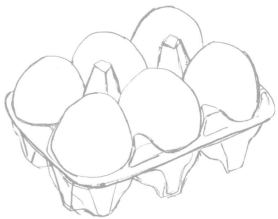

In this take on a Spanish tortilla, pieces of fried bread are used instead of potatoes. This omelette is great served with spinach salad and Roast Tomato Chutney (see page 181). The Hot Chilli Baked Tomatoes (below) go wonderfully with the Mexican Corn Cakes (see page 26), and are great as part of a mezze platter.

Brunch Bread & Chorizo Omelette

SERVES 4

1 tablespoon olive oil

75g (3oz) cured chorizo sausage, chopped

2 thick slices of dairy-free sourdough bread or focaccia, roughly chopped

6 free-range eggs

40g (1½oz) dairy-free Cheddar-style cheese, finely grated

salt and pepper

Preheat the grill to medium.

Heat the oil in a medium-sized, nonstick frying pan, add the chorizo and fry over a medium heat for 2 minutes. Add the bread, stir to mix well and cook for 2–3 minutes or until golden and crisp.

Break the eggs into a bowl, whisk together and season well.

Pour the eggs into the pan and cook for 2–3 minutes. Scatter over the cheese.

Place the pan under the grill for 2–3 minutes until the omelette is just set, golden and bubbling.

Hot Chilli Baked Tomatoes

SERVES 4

8 ripe vine tomatoes, separated from the vine but with the stalks left on

175g (6oz) slices of air-cured ham

2 tablespoons virgin olive oil

2 teaspoons sugar

2 large mild red chillies, deseeded and finely diced

Preheat the oven to 200°C/fan 180°C/400°F/Gas Mark 6.

Cut a small slice from the base of each tomato to allow them to stand upright.

Lay out the slices of air-cured ham, drizzle with the olive oil and sprinkle with the sugar and chillies. Carefully wrap each tomato in a slice of coated ham and place on a lipped baking sheet.

Bake the wrapped tomatoes for 15–20 minutes until they are soft but still holding their shape and the ham is crisp.

This is my simplified version of a traditional Mediterranean sandwich. It's perfect for outdoor brunch and it's also great for picnics, as it travels really well. You need to make this the day before to allow all the flavours to infuse and soak into the bread. I always bring along a little jar of extra balsamic vinegar and olive oil to drizzle over once the pan bagne is cut into thick wedges.

Pan Bagne

SERVES 6

4 tablespoons balsamic vinegar

1 garlic clove, crushed

7 tablespoons extra virgin olive oil

1 round, flat dairy-free granary or sourdough loaf, about 400g (13oz)

salt and pepper

FILLING

285g (9½oz) sunblush tomatoes, drained and roughly chopped

225g (7½oz) antipasti artichokes in oil, drained and roughly sliced

24 black olives, pitted

225g (7½oz) antipasti roasted peppers in oil, drained and roughly sliced

3 tablespoons baby capers, drained

1 large ripe avocado, halved, stoned, peeled and sliced

1 small bunch of basil leaves

For the dressing, mix together the balsamic vinegar, garlic and oil in a small bowl and season to taste with salt and pepper.

Slice the loaf horizontally into 3 layers.

Generously sprinkle each layer with the dressing. Set the top of the loaf to one side.

Scatter the bottom and middle layers of bread with the filling ingredients. Drizzle over the remaining dressing and reassemble the loaf.

Press the layers together well and wrap the loaf tightly in clingfilm. Place on a large plate and top with another 2–3 plates to help compress the loaf. Chill overnight before serving.

To serve, unwrap, place on a board and cut in half to reveal the filling. Using a large, serrated bread knife, carefully cut each half into thick wedges.

You don't need a juicer to make Beetroot Vodka Shots – there are some fabulous beetroot juices available. Make as spicy as you dare and serve over plenty of ice. This also works really well with gin. Serve with smoked salmon on rye toasts or Breakfast Bacon Popcorn (see below), which is easy to cook, fun to serve and incredibly moreish. Once the corn starts to pop, don't lift the lid – it's done when the popping sound stops.

Beetroot Vodka Shots

SERVES 4

200ml (7fl oz) vodka

900ml (1½ pints) beetroot juice

a few shakes of Tabasco sauce, or to taste

1 teaspoon celery salt

4 celery sticks

4 lime wedges

ice, to serve

Mix together the vodka, beetroot juice, Tabasco and celery salt in a large jug.

Pour into 4 tumblers half-filled with ice. Finish each glass with a celery stick and a lime wedge.

Breakfast Bacon Popcorn

SERVES 6

2 tablespoons sunflower oil

125g (4oz) smoked bacon lardons

2 tablespoons chopped rosemary

100g (3½oz) popping corn

Heat the oil in a large saucepan with a tight-fitting lid. Stir in the bacon lardons and cook for 3 minutes or until golden. Stir in half the rosemary.

Remove the pan from the heat, add the popcorn maize and cover with the lid. Place the pan back over a medium heat for 2–3 minutes. You will start to hear the corn pop loudly. Shake the pan occasionally until the sound of corn popping has stopped.

Stir in the remaining rosemary and tip out into a serving bowl. Serve straight away.

These scrummy sweetcorn cakes topped with a creamy avocado crush make a feast of Mexican and Mediterranean flavours when served with Hot Chilli Baked Tomatoes (see page 22). I like to add warm taco chips on the side too.

Mexican Corn Cakes with Avocado Crush

SERVES 4

100g (3½ oz) self-raising flour

1 teaspoon baking powder

275g (9oz) drained canned sweetcorn in water

2 large free-range eggs, beaten

150ml (½ pint) dairy-free milk

2 tablespoons olive oil

pepper

AVOCADO CRUSH

2 ripe avocados, halved, stoned, peeled and cut into small chunks

juice of 1 lime

1 garlic clove, crushed

2 shallots, finely chopped

8 cherry tomatoes, quartered

1 large red chilli, deseeded and finely chopped

2 tablespoons extra virgin olive oil

salt and pepper

To make the avocado crush, place the avocado in a bowl and squeeze over the lime juice. Gently mix in the other crush ingredients and season to taste with salt and pepper. Set to one side.

Sift together the flour and baking powder into a large bowl and season with a little pepper. Add the sweetcorn, eggs and milk and quickly mix together to form a loose batter.

Heat 1 tablespoon of the oil in a large, nonstick frying pan. Spoon 3 heaps of the mixture into the pan and gently press out to form 3 rough thick rounds. Fry over a medium heat for 2–3 minutes until golden, then flip over and cook for a further 1–2 minutes until golden and cooked. Remove from the pan and keep warm in a low oven while you cook the remaining corn cakes.

To serve, pile the corn cakes on a board, then spoon the avocado crush into a serving bowl and place next to them.

Breakfast with a zing – these sizzling tomatoes with an extra bite of chilli and balsamic vinegar will soon get you going. If you can't face chilli in the morning, try scattering the tomatoes with a little basil, or omit the balsamic and sprinkle over the more traditional Worcestershire sauce. Serve them my favourite way as below, with toasted dairy-free rye or sourdough bread and a poached egg.

Spiked Balsamic Beef Tomatoes with Crispy Ham & Poached Egg

SERVES 4

4 beef tomatoes, halved

1 teaspoon chilli flakes

1 teaspoon caster sugar

2 tablespoons olive oil

70g (2¾oz) slices of air-cured ham

pepper

TO SERVE

4 slices of dairy-free rye or sourdough bread

4 very fresh free-range eggs

1 tablespoon white wine vinegar

2 tablespoons balsamic vinegar

Preheat the oven to 200°C/fan 180°C/400°F/Gas Mark 6. Place the tomatoes cut side up on a baking sheet.

Mix together the chilli flakes, sugar and 1½ tablespoons of the oil in a jug, then drizzle over the tomato halves. Grind over plenty of black pepper.

Bake for 12–15 minutes until the tomatoes are cooked through but still keeping their shape.

Meanwhile, heat the remaining oil in a frying pan over a medium heat and fry the ham for about 1 minute on each side or until crispy. Toast the bread.

For the perfect poached egg, first start with really fresh eggs. Bring a shallow saucepan filled two-thirds with water to a simmer and add the white wine vinegar. Crack each egg into a small cup and gently tip into the lightly simmering water. Allow the eggs to settle and cook for about 2–3 minutes until just set. They will eventually float to the top. Lift out the cooked eggs with a slotted spoon and rest the spoon briefly on kitchen paper to remove the excess water. Gently slide each poached egg on to a slice of toast on a warmed serving plate and season with pepper.

Divide the tomatoes among the plates and drizzle each with a little balsamic vinegar. Top with the crispy ham and serve straight away.

Big
Salads
& Super
Soups

This summer salad is fab with canned tuna in olive oil, or if you want to be more extravagant, try it with fresh griddled tuna steaks. If fish isn't your thing, then serve it with griddled chicken or crispy air-cured ham.

Tuscan Bread & Tomato Salad with Sweet Peppers & Black Olives

SERVES 4

4 thick slices of dairy-free sourdough bread or focaccia

3 tablespoons extra virgin olive oil, plus extra for drizzling

1 garlic clove, crushed

250g (8oz) baby plum tomatoes, halved

1 large red pepper, cored, deseeded and diced

100g (3½ oz) mixed black and green olives, pitted and torn in half

2 tablespoons baby capers, drained and rinsed

1 small red onion, finely chopped

1 mild red chilli, deseeded and finely chopped

1 small bunch of basil

2 x 120g (4oz) cans good-quality tuna in olive oil, drained and flaked

salt and pepper

Preheat the oven to 210°C/fan 190°C/425°F/Gas Mark 7.

Tear the bread into large bite-sized pieces and place in a bowl. Mix half the oil and garlic together and drizzle over the bread. Toss together until well coated.

Transfer the bread to a baking sheet and bake for 12–15 minutes or until golden and crisp.

Meanwhile, toss together the tomatoes, red pepper, olives, capers, onion, chilli and remaining olive oil in a large bowl. Season well with salt and pepper.

Add the warm croutons to the tomato mixture with two-thirds of the basil and gently mix.

To serve, spoon the salad into a mound into the centre of each serving bowl and top each with flakes of tuna, the remaining basil leaves, a drizzle of olive oil and pepper.

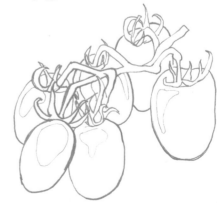

*Coleslaw can be a sensational salad or side dish – delicious and crisp.
You will need really fresh broccoli here to make the grating easy.*

Broccoli Coleslaw

SERVES 6

1 head of broccoli, about 500g (1lb)

1 fennel bulb, trimmed and finely sliced

2 garlic cloves, crushed

1 large red onion, finely chopped

4 tablespoons dairy-free mayonnaise

juice of 1 lime

salt and pepper

Cut the broccoli into large florets, including some of the stalk. Grate on the large side of a hand grater and place in a bowl.

Add the fennel, garlic and red onion to the grated broccoli and mix together well.

Add the mayonnaise and lime juice and toss together, then season to taste with salt and pepper.

It only takes a few minutes to put this colourful warm salad together.

Asparagus with Tomato & Pea Dressing

SERVES 4

2 bunches of young asparagus, trimmed

4 tablespoons olive oil, plus extra for drizzling

1½ tablespoons cold water

250g (8oz) baby plum or cherry tomatoes, halved

100g (3½oz) frozen peas, defrosted

2 tablespoons balsamic vinegar

2 tablespoons pine nuts, toasted

pepper

Wash the asparagus and place the wet asparagus with half the oil in a bowl. Grind over some black pepper and toss together well.

Heat a large, nonstick frying pan until hot, add the asparagus and fry for 2 minutes. Reduce the heat, then add the measurement water, cover with a lid and cook for a further 3–4 minutes or until the asparagus is just tender. Remove the asparagus from the pan and divide among 4 warmed serving plates.

Add the remaining oil to the frying pan and increase the heat to high. Add the tomatoes to the pan and cook for 1 minute, then add the peas and cook for a further 2 minutes or until heated through. Drizzle over the balsamic vinegar and shake the pan to coat the tomatoes.

Spoon the tomatoes and peas and any juices over the asparagus. Scatter over the pine nuts, drizzle over a little extra olive oil and grind over black pepper, then serve straight away with warm crusty bread.

This delicious salad is so quick and easy to prepare. Toasting the bread keeps it crispy and adds a real crunch to the salad. The secret of this simple salad is to cook the poached egg until just soft so that it can ooze all over the dressed leaves.

Bacon & Croute Salad with Chilli & Leek Poached Egg

SERVES 4

2 large slices of rustic dairy-free bread, such as focaccia or sourdough

3 tablespoons extra virgin olive oil

1 leek, trimmed, cleaned and very finely shredded into strips

1 red chilli, deseeded and cut into slivers

splash of balsamic vinegar

8 streaky bacon rashers

1 tablespoon white wine vinegar

4 very fresh free-range eggs

about 100g (3½oz) bag mixed salad leaves

pepper

Preheat the oven to 200°C/fan 180°C/400°F/Gas Mark 6. Preheat the grill to high.

Tear the bread into bite-sized pieces and place in a bowl. Add half the oil and toss together until well coated.

Transfer the bread to a baking sheet and bake for 8 minutes or until golden and crisp.

Meanwhile, heat the remaining oil in a small saucepan. Add the leek and chilli and gently fry for 1–2 minutes until softened. Stir in the balsamic vinegar.

Grill the bacon for 5–6 minutes until crispy, turning once.

For the poached eggs, bring a shallow saucepan filled two-thirds with water to a simmer and add the white wine vinegar. Crack each egg into a small cup and gently tip into the lightly simmering water. Allow the eggs to settle and cook for about 2–3 minutes until just set. They will eventually float to the top. Lift out the cooked eggs with a slotted spoon and rest the spoon briefly on kitchen paper to remove the excess water.

To serve, transfer the leeks and chilli to a large bowl and toss with the salad leaves and crisp croutons. Divide among 4 serving plates. Top each plate with a poached egg and grind over a little black pepper. Top each serving with 2 pieces of crispy bacon and serve at once.

Ham and chips gets poshed up with a zingy balsamic and lentil dressing. This dressing is also delicious served with grilled fish, seafood or roast chicken or simply drizzled over roasted veggies. Don't be tempted to use canned lentils here, as they are too soft.

Chunky Chip Salad with Ham Hock & Puy Lentil Dressing

SERVES 4

875g (1¾ lb) potatoes, washed but unpeeled

2 tablespoons olive oil

175g (6oz) cooked ham hock, flaked

90g (3½oz) pea shoots or mixed salad leaves

1 quantity of Balsamic & Puy Lentil Dressing (see below)

salt and pepper

BALSAMIC & PUY LENTIL DRESSING

3 tablespoons cooked Puy lentils

2 tablespoons balsamic vinegar

5 tablespoons extra virgin olive oil

1 garlic clove, crushed

4 sun-dried tomatoes in oil, drained and chopped

salt and pepper

Preheat the oven to 200°C/fan 180°C/400°F/Gas Mark 6. Line a roasting tin with baking parchment.

Trim the potatoes into squares and cut each into 1.5-cm (¾-inch) chunky chips.

Place the chips in the lined tin, add the oil and toss to coat. Season well with salt and pepper.

Bake for 35–40 minutes or until cooked through and golden.

Meanwhile, for the balsamic and puy lentil dressing, place all the ingredients in a small bowl and gently mix together. Season to taste with salt and pepper.

Toss the ham hock and pea shoots together and pile a mound on each serving plate. Top each with a pile of chunky chips and drizzle over the dressing.

Add an interesting twist to noodles with a dressing of ginger, orange and sesame. These fresh, sweet and aromatic flavours just pop in the mouth. This salad is also great served with grilled salmon or tuna.

Noodle Salad with Crispy Duck Legs

SERVES 4

4 duck legs

2 teaspoons sea salt

125g (4oz) sugar snap peas

200g (7oz) medium egg noodles

125g (4oz) spring greens, shredded

2 large carrots, peeled and then peeled into ribbons with a vegetable peeler

6 spring onions, finely sliced

1 bunch of coriander leaves

1 quantity of Warm Ginger & Orange Sesame Dressing (see page 182)

salt

Preheat the oven to 200°C/fan 180°C/400°F/Gas Mark 6.

Using a small, sharp knife, prick the duck legs all over. Place on a wire rack set over a roasting tin. Rub salt all over the duck legs and roast for about 45–50 minutes until crispy and cooked through.

Meanwhile, cook the noodles according to the packet instructions, then drain.

Blanch the sugar snap peas in a saucepan of boiling water for 1 minute, then drain and refresh under cold running water. Halve lengthways.

Blanch and refresh the spring greens in the same way. Drain well.

Toss together the noodles, sugar snap peas, spring greens, carrots, spring onions and half the coriander leaves in a bowl. Add the warm dressing and toss to coat.

Once the duck is cooked, remove from the oven. To shred the duck, use 2 forks to remove the crispy skin and meat from each leg. Pile some noodle salad into each serving bowl, top with the crispy duck and scatter over the remaining coriander. Serve straight away.

If you've never had pineapple this way, you've got to try this recipe. It's a real showstopper – I love to present it as a huge rustic board, put it in the middle of the table and let everyone help themselves. You can use cold leftover chicken in place of the smoked, and the pineapple also makes a great pud served with crumbly meringues and your favourite dairy-free ice cream or sorbet.

Pineapple & Smoked Chicken Sambal

SERVES 4

1 large, sweet ripe pineapple

1 red chilli, deseeded and finely chopped

2 tablespoons clear honey

juice of 2 oranges

100g (3½oz) raw cashew nuts, toasted and chopped

4 spring onions, finely chopped

2 tablespoons chopped coriander

1 tablespoon extra virgin olive oil

150g (5oz) cooked smoked chicken, finely shredded

salt and pepper

Cut the top and bottom off the pineapple and cut away all the skin including the 'eyes', then quarter and remove the core from each wedge. Cut each wedge in half, giving 8 wedges in total.

Place the pineapple wedges in a bowl and add the chilli, honey and orange juice. Toss well and set aside for 10 minutes to marinate.

Meanwhile, mix the cashew nuts, spring onions, coriander and olive oil together in a bowl, season to taste with salt and pepper and set to one side.

Heat a griddle pan over a medium heat. Remove the pineapple wedges from the marinade, reserving the marinade, and add to the pan. Cook for 2–3 minutes on each side or until lightly charred.

Arrange the pineapple on a large rustic board, then top with the chicken and scatter over the cashew nut relish.

Pour the reserved marinade into the hot griddle pan and allow it to bubble off the heat for a few seconds until syrupy, then drizzle over the finished dish.

Don't be put off by the long list of ingredients here. This salad can use any leftovers you have to hand – cold chicken, cold new potatoes, salami and air-cured meats, antipasti artichokes or aubergines and any salad leaves you fancy. Present it on a large rustic-style board for full effect, and it's great with the Soured Cream & Tarragon Dressing (see page 183) or the Smoked Garlic & Chive Mayo (see page 185). Traditionally this salad is served with potatoes and anchovy fillets too, but I prefer to serve it with the Caramelized Onion & Spelt Flatbread (see page 136) or the Thyme, Garlic & Chilli Socca (see page 139).

Niçoise Rustic Board

SERVES 6

225g (7½oz) green beans, topped and tailed

3 peppered smoked mackerel fillets, skinned

2 skinless smoked trout fillets

1 tablespoon balsamic vinegar

3 tablespoons extra virgin olive oil

1 small red onion, finely chopped

3 large ripe plum tomatoes, roughly chopped

2 heads of white or red chicory, each cut into 4 wedges

340g (11½ oz) jar antipasti roasted peppers in oil, drained

250g (8oz) mixed olives

125g (4oz) frisée (curly endive) lettuce leaves

4 free-range eggs, hard-boiled, shelled and halved

salt and pepper

Cook the green beans in a saucepan of boiling water for 3–4 minutes until just tender, then drain, refresh under cold water and pat dry. Set to one side.

Pull the fish into large flakes and set to one side.

Mix the balsamic vinegar, olive oil and red onion together in a small bowl. Season well with salt and pepper.

Place the green beans and tomatoes separately in small bowls. Divide the dressing between each and toss well. Set to one side.

Arrange the flaked fish, chicory, peppers, olives, frisée and egg halves in clusters on the board. Add the dressed green beans and tomatoes. Take to the table with the dressing of your choice and warm bread, and allow everyone to help themselves.

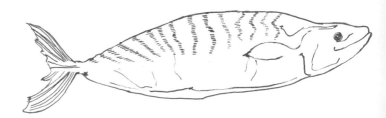

I know it's not a chefy thing to admit, but give me purple sprouting broccoli in place of asparagus any day! This vibrant, hearty soup with Mediterranean crumbly croutes is a real taste sensation. If you have ardent meat lovers in the family, simply fry off a little chopped chorizo and scatter with the croutes.

Purple Sprouting Broccoli Soup with Tapenade Croutes

SERVES 4

2 tablespoons olive oil

1 onion, finely chopped

1 red chilli, kept whole

450g (14½oz) purple sprouting broccoli, trimmed

175g (6oz) frozen peas

1 litre (1¾ pints) hot vegetable stock

100ml (3½fl oz) dairy-free single cream

salt and pepper

TAPENADE CROUTES

1 small dairy-free focaccia loaf, torn into bite-sized pieces

extra virgin olive oil, for drizzling

12 green olives, pitted and chopped

1 small bunch of basil, leaves torn

Preheat the oven to 200°C/fan 180°C/400°F/Gas Mark 6.

Heat the oil in a saucepan, add the onion and cook gently for 5 minutes until softened.

Add the chilli, broccoli, peas and hot stock and bring to the boil, then reduce the heat and simmer for 6 minutes.

Remove the chilli from the soup, split in half and remove the seeds and stalk. Transfer the soup to a blender with the chilli and whizz until smooth.

Return the soup to a clean pan and stir in the cream. Season to taste with salt and pepper and heat through gently.

Meanwhile, for the tapenade croutes, place the focaccia on a baking sheet, drizzle with olive oil and bake for 8 minutes or until golden and crisp.

Toss the toasted focaccia with the olives and torn basil leaves.

Ladle the soup into warmed serving bowls and top with the tapenade croutes. Drizzle with a little extra olive oil and serve straight away.

This delicately spiced soup is really rich and creamy. But the thing that makes it extra special is the nutty topping of roasted cashews spiced with aromatic cardamom.

Parsnip & Chilli Soup with Cardamom Crumbs

SERVES 6

2 tablespoons olive oil

1 onion, chopped

1 small leek, trimmed, cleaned and chopped

1 red chilli, kept whole

750g parsnips (1½lb), peeled and chopped

grated rind of 1 unwaxed lime

1 litre (1¾ pints) vegetable stock

2 tablespoons dairy-free single cream, plus extra, to serve (optional)

salt and pepper

CRUMBS

2 tablespoons rapeseed oil

7 cardamom pods, crushed and husks discarded

125g (4oz) dairy-free fresh white breadcrumbs

40g (1½oz) salted roasted cashew nuts, finely chopped

Heat the oil in a saucepan, add the onion, leek and chilli and cook gently for 5 minutes until softened. Add the parsnips and lime rind, stir well and cook for 2 minutes.

Add the stock and bring to the boil, then reduce the heat and simmer for 15–20 minutes.

Remove the chilli from the soup, split in half and remove the seeds and stalk. Transfer the soup to a blender with the chilli and whizz until smooth.

Return the soup to a clean pan and stir in the cream, if using. Season to taste with salt and pepper and heat through gently.

To make the crumbs, heat the rapeseed oil in a large, nonstick frying pan, stir in the cardamom seeds and cook over a medium heat for 30 seconds. Add the breadcrumbs and cashews and fry, stirring frequently, for 5 minutes until golden and crispy.

Serve the soup topped with the crispy crumbs and dairy-free cream, if liked.

This broth has aromatic spice, heat and freshness. Cauliflower is often seen as mundane, but teamed here with cashews, spinach and spice, it's anything but. Use this Thai broth as a base for all Thai-style curries such as fish, shellfish, chicken, beef or pork.

Thai Broth with Crispy Noodles

SERVES 4

400ml (14fl oz) can coconut milk

300ml (½ pint) vegetable stock

450g (14½oz) cauliflower florets

sunflower oil, for deep-frying

125g (4oz) rice noodles

50g (2oz) spinach, roughly shredded

100g (3½oz) raw cashew nuts, toasted

coriander leaves, for scattering

CURRY PASTE

2 tablespoons sunflower oil

50g (2oz) fresh root ginger, peeled and chopped

1 lemon grass stalk, bruised and roughly chopped

1 green chilli, halved, deseeded and chopped

1 red chilli, halved, deseeded and chopped

1 large garlic clove, crushed

1 small bunch of coriander, stalks and leaves

3 spring onions, roughly chopped

Place all the curry paste ingredients and 2 tablespoons of the coconut milk in a small food processor and whizz together until smooth.

Heat a wok or large frying pan, add the paste and cook over a medium heat, stirring constantly, for 2 minutes.

Add the remaining coconut milk and stock and bring to the boil. Add the cauliflower florets to the broth, reduce the heat and simmer for 8–10 minutes until just cooked.

Heat the oil for deep-frying in a deep-fat fryer or deep saucepan to 180–190°C (350–375°F), or until a cube of bread browns in 30 seconds. Add the noodles to the hot oil in small batches and fry for 30 seconds until golden and crisp. Remove, draining off the excess oil, and transfer to kitchen paper to drain further.

Add the spinach to the broth and simmer for a further 30 seconds. Stir in the cashew nuts.

To serve, ladle the Thai broth into 4 warmed serving bowls. Place some crisp-fried noodles on top of each and a scattering of coriander leaves. Serve straight away.

Soups are so simple and offer a speedy, tasty and nutritious meal. I love to add a little sexiness, such as the Fresh Chilli Relish used here. It's also fab as an accompaniment to curry or shellfish.

Spiced Sweet Potato Chowder

SERVES 4

2 tablespoons shop-bought curry paste, such as Madras or korma if you like it milder

1 onion, finely chopped

350g (11½oz) potatoes, peeled and cut into 1.5-cm (¾-inch) cubes

1 large sweet potato, peeled and cut into 1.5-cm (¾-inch) cubes

175g (6oz) dried red split lentils, washed

900ml (1½ pints) vegetable stock

150ml (¼ pint) coconut cream, plus extra for drizzling

salt and pepper

FRESH CHILLI RELISH

½ bunch of spring onions, finely chopped

1 red chilli, deseeded and finely chopped

1 small bunch of flat leaf parsley, leaves picked

squeeze of lime juice

2 teaspoons olive oil

Heat a saucepan, add the curry paste and cook over a medium heat, stirring constantly, for 2 minutes. Stir in the onion, cover with a lid and steam-fry for 5 minutes, stirring occasionally.

Add the potatoes, sweet potato, lentils and stock to the pan. Bring to the boil, then reduce the heat and simmer for 20 minutes or until the potatoes are just tender.

Meanwhile, for the fresh chilli relish, simply toss all the ingredients together in a bowl and then spoon into a serving bowl. Set to one side.

Stir 150ml (¼ pint) of the coconut cream into the soup and season to taste with salt and pepper. Stir a little extra coconut cream in a small bowl until smooth.

Ladle the soup into warmed bowls. Using a spoon, drizzle in a little extra coconut cream and top with the Fresh Chilli Relish. Serve with mango chutney and poppadums.

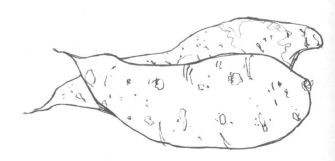

I don't know why barley is such an underrated grain; maybe it's just because it sounds rather old-fashioned. But here it is the hero grain! It has a delicious nutty flavour and creates a lovely, creamy texture once cooked. Use in soups, stews and risotto-like dishes. Any leftovers can be reheated risotto style and served with your favourite sausages or pork chops with a good dollop of mustard.

Barley Minestrone with Broad Bean & Basil Pistou

SERVES 4

1.5 litres (2½ pints) chicken or vegetable stock

100g (3½oz) dried pearl barley

2 tablespoons olive oil

1 leek, trimmed, cleaned and finely chopped

2 celery sticks, finely chopped

2 large carrots, peeled and finely chopped

1 parsnip, peeled and finely chopped

2 bay leaves

1 tablespoon thyme leaves

2 tablespoons sun-dried tomato paste

5 tablespoons white wine

2 tablespoons chopped parsley

salt and pepper

4 tablespoons Broad Bean & Basil Pistou or Classic Pesto (see page 184), to serve

Pour the stock into a large bowl, add the pearl barley and set aside for 30 minutes.

Heat the oil in a large saucepan, add the leek, celery, carrots, parsnip, bay and thyme and cook over a medium heat for 5 minutes.

Stir in tomato paste and cook for 3 minutes. Pour in the wine and the stock and pearl barley and bring to the boil, then reduce the heat and simmer for 15–20 minutes.

Stir in the parsley and season to taste with salt and pepper. Pour into warmed bowls and serve with the pistou or pesto.

It's fast, it's healthy and best of all it's really tasty! Blitzing half the potatoes with the soya milk and stock really makes this chowder creamy without having to add any cream. Serve with warm Bacon & Sage Cornbread (see page 142) or Chive & Cheese Soda Bread (see page 142).

Creamy Corn & Haddock Chowder

SERVES 4

1 tablespoon olive oil	Heat the oil in a large saucepan, add the onion and cook for 5 minutes. Add the potatoes and cook for a further minute.
1 onion, finely chopped	
500g (1lb) potatoes, peeled and cut into 1.5-cm (¾-in) cubes	Pour in the stock, cover with a lid and simmer for 12–15 minutes or until the potatoes are tender. Using a slotted spoon, remove half the potatoes from the stock and set to one side.
600ml (1 pint) fish or vegetable stock	
300ml (½ pint) soya milk	Place the remaining potatoes, stock and soya milk in a blender and carefully blitz until smooth. Pour back into the pan.
250g (8oz) canned sweetcorn in water, drained	
450g (14½oz) skinless undyed smoked haddock or cod fillets, cut into bite-sized pieces	Add the sweetcorn and simmer for 2 minutes. Stir in the smoked fish and reserved potatoes and cook for a further 3–4 minutes. Stir in the parsley and season to taste with salt and pepper.
2 tablespoon chopped parsley	
salt and pepper	Ladle into 4 warmed bowls and serve straight away.

Frozen peas are a must in the freezer so that you can whip up this creamy chowder whenever you want. Serve with garlic bread or try it with the super-speedy Skillet Scones (see below).

Pea & Bacon Chowder

SERVES 4

1 tablespoon olive oil

1 onion, finely chopped

1 garlic clove, crushed

680g (1lb 6oz) frozen petit pois

750ml (1¼ pints) vegetable stock

salt and pepper

TO SERVE

8 streaky bacon rashers

handful of rocket leaves

Heat the oil in a saucepan, add the onion and cook over a medium heat for 5–6 minutes until softened. Add the garlic and cook for a further minute.

Stir in three-quarters of the petit pois and pour in the stock. Bring to the boil, then reduce the heat and simmer for 10–12 minutes. Transfer to a blender or food processor and whizz until smooth.

Return the soup to the pan and add the remaining petit pois. Bring to the boil and then simmer for 2 minutes. Season to taste.

Meanwhile, preheat the grill to high. Grill the bacon until crisp.

Ladle the soup into warmed bowls and top with bacon and rocket leaves.

Skillet Scones

SERVES 4

300g (10oz) plain flour, plus extra for dusting

1½ tablespoons baking powder

50ml (2fl oz) rapeseed or olive oil

1 tablespoon almond milk (see page 177 for homemade)

1 egg, beaten

150ml (½ pint) dairy-free single cream

2 tablespoons chopped parsley

salt and pepper

Sift the flour and baking powder into a large bowl. Season well.

Mix together half the oil, the almond milk, egg and dairy-free cream in a large jug, then stir in the parsley. Pour the wet ingredients into the dry and gently combine to form a soft and manageable dough.

Gently roll out the dough on a lightly floured surface into a 15-cm (6-inch) round about 1.5cm (¾ inch) thick. Cut out into 8 wedges.

Place a large, nonstick frying pan over a medium heat and add the remaining oil. Add the scones to the pan and cook for about 8–10 minutes on each side until browned and cooked through. Serve warm.

Weekday Favourites

Simply take this dish of delicious, spicy everyday veggies topped with eggs and wilted spinach to the table in the pan it's cooked in and serve straight away. You will need a really good nonstick frying pan for this recipe.

Pan-fried Vegetable Bhaji with Eggs & Wilted Greens

SERVES 4

4 tablespoons medium curry paste, such as Madras or rogan josh

450g (14½oz) potatoes, peeled and grated

2 leeks, trimmed, cleaned and finely shredded

2 carrots, peeled and grated

1 tablespoon coconut oil

4 free-range eggs

large handful of baby spinach leaves, finely shredded

salt and pepper

Heat a small saucepan, add the curry paste and cook over a medium heat, stirring constantly, for 3 minutes to bring out the flavours.

With your hands, squeeze out as much liquid as possible from the grated potatoes. Place them in a large bowl with the leeks and carrots. Stir in the curry paste, season well with salt and pepper and toss everything together until the veggies are thoroughly coated – to be honest, I normally use my hands for this.

Preheat the grill to medium.

Spoon the coconut oil into a large, nonstick frying pan, add the vegetables and make 4 indentations in the top of the bhaji. Cook over a medium heat for 10 minutes until golden underneath.

Place the pan under the grill and cook for 8–10 minutes or until the bhaji is golden on top. Remove from the grill.

Crack and pour an egg into each indentation and grind over a little black pepper. Place back over a medium heat on the hob, cover with a lid and cook for about 5–6 minutes or until the eggs are cooked to your liking.

Scatter over the spinach and take to the table to serve.

I promise you that once you've made hummus with butter beans instead of chickpeas, there is no going back. The nutty spice mix Dukkah is good to serve alongside – dip the bread first in the oil and then into the Dukkah.

White Bean Creamy Hummus with Broad Bean Salad & Dukkah

SERVES 4

410g (13½oz) can butter beans, drained and rinsed

4 tablespoons tahini paste

1 garlic clove, roughly chopped

juice of 1 lemon

8 tablespoons olive oil

2 tablespoons warm water

1 small bunch of flat leaf parsley, leaves picked

100g (3½oz) skinned cooked broad beans

2 tablespoons pine nuts, toasted

½ teaspoon chilli flakes

DUKKAH

2 tablespoons sesame seeds

1 tablespoon cumin seeds

½ tablespoon ground coriander

25g (1oz) whole blanched almonds, toasted

TO SERVE

4 flatbreads, warmed

1 large bunch of radishes, trimmed

olive oil, for dipping

Place the butter beans, tahini paste and garlic in a food processor and whizz until smooth.

Add the lemon juice, 6 tablespoons of the oil and the measurement water, then whizz again until very smooth. Season to taste with salt and pepper.

Mix together the parsley, broad beans, pine nuts and chilli flakes in a bowl. Set to one side.

For the Dukkah, toast the sesame seeds, cumin seeds and ground coriander in a dry frying pan for 2 minutes.

Place the almonds in a food processor with the toasted spices and season with salt and pepper. Pulse for just a few seconds until medium ground.

To serve, spread the hummus on to 4 serving plates. Scatter over the broad bean salad and drizzle each with the remaining oil. Serve with the warm flatbreads and crunchy radishes, together with the Dukkah for dipping.

Store the Dukkah in a sterilized Kilner or other preserving jar or jam jar in a cool, dark place – it will keep for up to 4 weeks in an airtight container. It makes a great crust for roasting salmon or chicken, or sprinkle it over your fave salad or homemade soups.

The very simplest, tastiest pasta dish, this is also a real storecupboard saviour. Crispy crumbs and pasta may sound a bit bonkers, but I promise you it really works.

Basil & Bean Linguine with Crispy Crumbs

SERVES 4

350g (11½oz) dried linguine

8 tablespoons extra virgin olive oil

4 tablespoons focaccia or dairy-free fresh white breadcrumbs

2 red chillies, deseeded and finely chopped

2 garlic cloves, crushed

1 large bunch of basil leaves

2 x 400g (13oz) cans borlotti beans, drained and rinsed

juice of 1 lemon

salt and pepper

Cook the pasta according to the packet instructions.

Meanwhile, heat 2 tablespoons of the oil in a medium-sized frying pan, stir in the breadcrumbs and cook over a medium heat for about 5 minutes until golden and crisp. Transfer to a small bowl.

Return the pan to a medium heat, add the remaining oil, the chillies, garlic and basil and cook for 30 seconds or until the basil turns bright green. Throw in the beans and heat through. Add the lemon juice and season well with salt and pepper.

To serve, drain the cooked pasta and toss through the hot basil beans. Pile into 4 warmed serving bowls and scatter over the crispy crumbs. Grind over some black pepper and serve at once.

It doesn't get much easier than this! The size of the pan, however, is really important – it needs to have a wide base and be fairly shallow. For this dish you need good-quality, flavoursome ingredients. Good is simple; simple is good!

Altogether Pasta Pronto

SERVES 4

3 tablespoons extra virgin olive oil

325g (11oz) dried tagliatelle

450g (14½oz) large ripe plum tomatoes, roughly chopped

1 bunch of spring onions, roughly chopped

3 large garlic cloves, crushed

1 teaspoon chilli flakes

1 litre (1¾ pints) water

1 small bunch of basil leaves, torn

salt and pepper

Add 2 tablespoons of the oil to a large sauté pan, then arrange the tagliatelle nests in the pan in a single layer. Scatter over the tomatoes, spring onions, garlic and chilli flakes. Pour over the measurement water and season really well with salt and pepper.

Place over a high heat, cover with a lid and bring to the boil. Remove the lid once boiling and cook over a high heat for 10–12 minutes, tossing the pasta regularly until it is al dente and the liquid has been almost all absorbed.

Stir through the basil leaves, season to taste with salt and pepper and drizzle over the remaining oil. Take in the pan to the table to serve.

For the times when only something cheesy will do, treat yourself to this tasty cheat's version of the well-loved classic. I have fond memories of mum's sliced tomatoes on top of this family favourite, but I've brought it right up to date by using roasted chillied vine tomatoes and crispy bacon.

Double-baked Mac & Cheese with Roasted Vine Tomatoes

SERVES 4

4 tablespoons olive oil

4 tablespoons plain flour

1 tablespoon Dijon mustard

900ml (1½ pints) soya milk

175g (6oz) dairy-free strong Cheddar-style cheese, finely grated

freshly grated nutmeg, to taste

300g (10oz) dried macaroni, cooked according to the packet instructions

3 tablespoons dairy-free fresh white breadcrumbs

400g (13oz) baby vine tomatoes, kept on the vine

chilli or olive oil, for drizzling (optional)

6 rindless smoked streaky bacon rashers

salt and pepper

Preheat the oven to 200°C/fan 180°C/400°F/Gas Mark 6.

Heat 3 tablespoons of the oil in a large saucepan, add the flour and mustard and cook over a medium heat for 30 seconds. Remove from the heat and add all the soya milk. Whisk well until all the lumps have gone, then return to heat and bring to the boil, stirring constantly. Simmer for 4–5 minutes until thickish and smooth.

Add three-quarters of the dairy-free cheese, remove from the heat and stir until melted. Season to taste with nutmeg and salt and pepper.

Stir the cooked macaroni into the sauce and transfer to a large or 2 medium-sized, shallow ovenproof dishes. Mix together the remaining cheese and the breadcrumbs and scatter over the dish.

Bake for about 15 minutes until golden and bubbling hot and a good crust has formed.

Remove the mac and cheese from the oven, lay the tomato vine over the top and drizzle with chilli or olive oil, if using, then return to the oven for a further 8–10 minutes.

Meanwhile, grill or fry the bacon until crisp.

Crumble the bacon over the mac and cheese and serve at once.

The pea purée flavoured with sweet basil is the special element in this dish. Not only does it taste divine and have a wonderful vibrant colour, but it makes the risotto super rich and velvety.

Summer Fresh Pea & Sunblush Risotto

SERVES 4 AS A STARTER
OR 2 AS A MAIN COURSE

PEA PURÉE

2 tablespoons olive oil

1 onion, finely chopped

175g (6oz) frozen petit pois

200ml (7fl oz) boiling water

25g (1oz) basil, stalks and leaves

salt and pepper

RISOTTO

20 sunblush tomatoes, drained and 2 tablespoons of the oil reserved

1 onion, finely chopped

2 garlic cloves, crushed

150g (5oz) risotto rice

150ml (¼ pint) white wine

1 tablespoon olive oil

750ml (1¼ pints) hot vegetable stock

175g (6oz) podded fresh peas

To make the pea purée, heat the olive oil in a medium-sized, shallow pan, add the onion and cook over a medium heat for 5 minutes or until softened.

Add the petit pois and the measurement water and season well with salt and pepper. Bring to the boil, cover with a lid and cook for 2 minutes. Stir in all the basil and cook for 1 minute.

Transfer the pea mixture to a blender and purée until smooth. Season to taste with salt and pepper and set to one side to cool.

To make the risotto, heat the sunblush tomato oil in a saucepan. Stir in the onion and cook for 5 minutes or until softened. Add the garlic and cook for a further 2 minutes.

Stir in the rice and cook for 1 minute. Pour in the white wine, add the oil and cook until absorbed.

Add half the hot stock, a ladleful at a time, stirring until each addition is almost all absorbed into the rice – this will take approximately 10 minutes. Add the peas and continue adding the remaining stock as before, until the rice is cooked but still al dente – this will take approximately 8–10 minutes. Season to taste with salt and pepper.

To serve, mix the pea purée into the risotto, spoon into warmed serving dishes and top with the sunblush tomatoes.

Chestnut mushrooms are the brown form of the common mushroom, and I think they always taste and look more interesting than the white sort. Large field mushrooms have a good woodland flavour that works wonderfully well with the dry sherry. Serve it on sourdough toasts with the crunchy walnut and rocket salad for real posh mushrooms on toast.

Mushroom Stroganoff with Walnuts & Rocket

SERVES 4

2 tablespoons olive oil

1 large garlic clove, crushed

500g (1lb) chestnut mushrooms, thickly sliced

350g (11½oz) flat field mushrooms, peeled and thickly sliced

1 tablespoon plain flour

150ml (¼ pint) dry sherry

200ml (7fl oz) vegetable stock, plus extra if needed

1 bunch of thyme, roughly chopped

150ml (¼ pint) dairy-free single cream

90g (3½oz) rocket leaves

75g (3oz) walnut halves, toasted and crumbled

drizzle of extra virgin olive oil

1 tablespoon good-quality balsamic vinegar

4 thick slices of dairy-free rustic or sourdough bread, toasted

salt and pepper

Heat the olive oil in a large frying pan or sauté pan, add the garlic and cook over a medium heat for 30 seconds. Add the mushrooms and cook over a high heat for 4–5 minutes or until coloured.

Sprinkle over the flour and cook for 1 minute. Stir in the sherry, stock and the thyme, season well with salt and pepper and simmer for 10–15 minutes.

Add the cream to the mushrooms and simmer for a further 5 minutes, adding extra stock if the stroganoff looks too thick – it should be the consistency of a thick gravy.

Toss the rocket leaves and walnuts with the extra virgin olive oil and balsamic vinegar in a bowl.

To serve, top the toasted sourdough with the stroganoff and serve with the rocket and walnut salad.

These delicious toasted melts will really hit the spot! This is one of my favourite flavour combinations: creamy cider and cheese topped with air-cured ham.

Welsh Rarebit Melts

SERVES 4

125g (4oz) dairy-free Cheddar-style cheese, finely grated

3 teaspoons English mustard

2 tablespoons cider or white wine

5 tablespoons dairy-free single cream

8 large slices of dairy-free sourdough bread, about 1.5cm (¾inch) thick

1 red onion, finely sliced

3 tablespoons olive oil, plus extra if needed

4 slices of air-cured ham

90g (3½oz) rocket leaves

Preheat the oven to 200°C/fan 180°C/400°F/Gas Mark 6.

Mix together the cheese, mustard, cider or white wine and cream in a bowl. Spread over 4 of the bread slices, scatter over the red onion and sandwich together with remaining bread slices. Cut each in half so that you end up with 8 melts.

Heat half the oil in a large, nonstick frying pan over a medium heat. Add 2 of the melts and cook for about 1–2 minutes on each side until golden. Transfer to a baking sheet. Repeat with the remaining melts, adding the remaining oil. Place the melts in the oven for about 4–5 minutes until oozy in the middle.

Meanwhile, place the air-cured ham in the pan, adding the remaining oil if necessary, and fry over a medium heat until crispy.

Toss the rocket with a little olive oil in a bowl.

To serve, place 2 melts on each serving plate and top with the crispy ham, with a side of lightly dressed rocket leaves.

*Here's a variation on paella using small pasta instead of rice,
which gives a lighter result. Simply take to the table in its pan and
serve family style with a pile of Garlic Toasts.*

Pasta Paella with Basil Ink

SERVES 4–6

6 tablespoons olive oil

1 large onion, chopped

3 teaspoons smoked paprika

300g (10oz) small dried pasta – I used chifferi rigati – or you could use macaroni

1.2 litres (2 pints) vegetable stock

250g (8oz) frozen baby broad beans

250g (8oz) cherry tomatoes, halved

1 large garlic clove, crushed

1 small bunch of basil

1 tablespoon cold water

200g (7oz) can albacore tuna steak in olive oil (or any other good-quality canned tuna), lightly drained

2 tablespoons baby capers, drained

salt and pepper

GARLIC TOASTS

4 thick-cut slices of dairy-free country bread

1 large garlic clove, peeled but kept whole

30ml (1fl oz) extra virgin olive oil

2 tablespoons chopped parsley

pepper

Heat 2 tablespoons of the oil in a large, shallow sauté pan, add the onion and gently fry until softened and lightly coloured. Stir in the paprika and cook for a further 2 minutes.

Add the pasta and half the stock, then season well with salt and pepper, cover with a lid and simmer for 10 minutes.

Remove the lid from the pan and stir in the broad beans, tomatoes and remaining stock. Bring to the boil, then re-cover, reduce the heat and simmer for a further 5–6 minutes.

Meanwhile, for the garlic toasts, preheat the grill to medium. Toast the bread on both sides. Remove the toast from the grill and, while hot, rub with the garlic clove. Drizzle over the oil, scatter over the parsley and season with pepper. Pile on to a serving board and set to one side.

To make the basil ink, place the remaining oil, garlic, basil and measurement water in a small blender and whizz until smooth. Season to taste with salt and pepper.

Scatter the tuna and capers over the pasta but do not stir. Drizzle over the basil ink, grind over a little black pepper and take to the table in its pan. Serve with the Garlic Toasts.

Fish pie in a flash! These light and delicate pies are so simple to put together, with the fish steaming in the stock, wine and cream. Use fresh, ready-made filo pastry and then any leftovers can be frozen for later use. Serve with Creamy Garlic Mash (opposite).

Fish Cachets

SERVES 4

2 tablespoons olive oil, plus extra for brushing

1 leek, trimmed, halved, cleaned and cut into thin strips

2 large carrots, peeled and cut into thin strips

200g (7oz) skinless salmon fillet, cut into 3-cm (1¼-inch) chunks

300g (10oz) white fish fillets, such as lemon sole, pollock, cod or haddock, skinned, any stray bones removed and cut into 3-cm (1¼-inch) chunks

100g (3½oz) cooked peeled prawns

150ml (¼ pint) fish stock

2 tablespoons white wine

4 tablespoons dairy-free single cream

4 sheets of fresh filo pastry

salt and pepper

Preheat the oven to 200°C/fan 180°C/400°F/Gas Mark 6.

Heat the oil in a frying pan and stir in the vegetables. Cook over a gentle heat for 4 minutes until softened but not coloured. Season to taste with salt and pepper and spoon equally among 4 small, ovenproof soup bowls. Set to one side to cool.

Divide the fish evenly on top of the vegetables and top with the prawns. Drizzle over the stock, wine and cream, and season well with salt and pepper.

Unroll the pastry and brush one sheet with oil. Cut in half, then slightly scrunch one half and lay over the top of the soup bowl, allowing it to drape over slightly. Scrunch the remaining half and place on top. Repeat with the remaining 3 soup bowls.

Place the bowls on a baking sheet and bake for about 20–25 minutes until the pastry is golden and crisp and the fish and sauce are bubbling hot. Serve straight away.

Roasting the garlic gives it a much softer, sweeter flavour and its richness gives the mash an almost buttery taste. See below for other flavour additions.

Creamy Garlic Mash

SERVES 4

2 whole garlic bulbs

875g (1¾lb) floury potatoes, such as Maris Piper or King Edward

about 150ml (¼ pint) dairy-free milk

2 tablespoons olive oil

salt and pepper

Preheat the oven to 200°C/fan 180°C/400°F/Gas Mark 6.

Wrap the garlic bulbs in foil, place on a baking sheet and roast for 30 minutes.

Meanwhile, peel the potatoes and cut into even 5-cm (2-inch) pieces. Place in a medium-sized saucepan, cover with cold water and add a pinch of salt.

Bring the potatoes to the boil, then reduce the heat and simmer for about 15–20 minutes or until tender. Drain the potatoes and immediately return to the saucepan. Mash over the heat for 30 seconds to evaporate any excess water.

Place the milk in a small saucepan and heat. Remove the garlic from the oven and, when cool enough to handle, carefully squeeze the pulp from the garlic cloves into the milk along with the olive oil. Mash together until smooth and stir through the mash. Season to taste with salt and pepper and serve. Alternatively, for a completely smooth mash, push the potatoes through a potato ricer, then stir in the garlic milk.

Creamy Mustard Mash
Omit the garlic and add 2 tablespoons wholegrain mustard or to taste and 3 tablespoons chopped parsley with the milk.

Creamy Horseradish Mash
Omit the garlic and add 3–4 tablespoons dairy-free creamed horseradish sauce with the milk. Top your mash with freshly chopped chives.

Creamy and rich with a touch of freshness with lemon and chives, this is a kind of deconstructed fish pie without all the fuss and using only one pan and one serving dish. It makes a great family weekday supper dish. These potatoes are also good served straight from the pan with baked ham or roast chicken.

Creamy Lemon Potatoes with Herby Salmon

SERVES 4

300ml (½ pint) almond milk (see page 177 for homemade) or other dairy-free milk

250ml (8fl oz) carton dairy-free single cream

grated rind of 1 unwaxed lemon and juice of ½

1 garlic clove, crushed

875g (1¾lb) potatoes, peeled and cut into about 2-cm (¾-in) cubes

4 skinless salmon fillets, about 140g (4½oz) each

1 tablespoon olive oil

1 small bunch of chives, chopped

225g (7½oz) frozen petit pois

salt and pepper

Preheat the oven to 200°C/fan 180°C/400°F/Gas Mark 6.

Place the milk, cream, lemon rind and garlic in a nonstick sauté pan and season generously with salt and pepper. Heat gently until just boiling.

Add the potatoes to the pan and bring back to the boil. Reduce the heat and simmer over a medium heat for about 20 minutes or until the potatoes are just tender and still holding their shape.

Meanwhile, place the salmon fillets in a bowl, drizzle over the lemon juice and oil and scatter over the chives, then season well with salt and pepper. Mix well to coat the salmon fillets.

Add the peas to the potatoes and gently stir through, then pour into a gratin dish. Lay the salmon fillets over the top and bake for 15 minutes until cooked through. Serve with a watercress salad.

This uncomplicated fish pie has a twist of chilli and turmeric... we love all things spicy at home, and this pie is a real winner with all the family. You can use this tasty mash on shepherd's pie or cottage pie too.

Fiery Fish Pie

SERVES 4–6

1.25kg (2½lb) potatoes, peeled and cut into even-sized chunks

625g (1¼lb) skinless salmon fillet, cut into 3–4-cm (1¼–1¾-inch) chunks

350g (11½oz) skinless cod fillet

450ml (¾ pint) fish stock

75ml (3fl oz) white wine

40g (1½oz) dairy-free spread

1 small onion, finely chopped

2–3 hot red chillies, deseeded and finely chopped

40g (1½oz) plain flour

250ml (8fl oz) carton dairy-free single cream

250g (8oz) cooked peeled tiger prawns

1 tablespoon olive oil

2 teaspoons ground turmeric

75ml (3fl oz) dairy-free milk, warmed

salt and pepper

Preheat the oven to 210°C/fan 190°C/425°F/Gas Mark 7.

Place the potatoes in a large saucepan of cold water and bring to the boil, then reduce the heat and simmer for 20 minutes or until tender.

Meanwhile, place the salmon and cod in a large, shallow saucepan. Pour over the stock and white wine and bring to the boil, then reduce the heat, cover with a lid and simmer for 5 minutes. Remove the fish and transfer to a 2-litre (3½-pint) ovenproof or gratin dish. Strain the cooking liquid and set to one side.

Melt the spread in a saucepan. Add the onion and chillies and cook gently for 5 minutes or until softened but not coloured. Stir in the flour and cook for 1 minute. Gradually whisk in the reserved cooking liquid and simmer for 5 minutes.

Stir in the cream and prawns and cook for 2 minutes. Season to taste with salt and pepper and pour over the fish.

Drain the potatoes well. Tip back into the pan over a low heat, then mash, adding the oil, turmeric and milk. Season to taste with salt and pepper.

Spoon the mash over the fish and mark the surface with a fork. Bake for 25–30 minutes until golden and bubbling hot. Serve with mangetout, green beans or broccoli.

Rich, oily fish like mackerel works really well with Indian-style spices. To release the flavour from your coriander seeds, place in a plastic bag and bash with a rolling pin – it's worth the extra effort.

Cracked Coriander Griddled Mackerel Fillets with Spiced Orange Lentils

SERVES 4

2 tablespoons coriander seeds, crushed

1 tablespoon coarsely ground black pepper

4 tablespoons roughly chopped flat leaf parsley

8 small mackerel fillets

1 tablespoon olive oil

LENTILS

1 tablespoon sunflower oil

1 large onion, chopped

4 garlic cloves, crushed

1 tablespoon garam masala

350g (11½oz) dried orange lentils, washed

1.2 litres (2 pints) vegetable stock

225g (7½oz) spinach leaves, roughly chopped

RELISH

1 large red onion, finely chopped

2 large ripe tomatoes, finely chopped

1 tablespoon chopped mint leaves

squeeze of lemon juice

salt and pepper

Mix together the crushed coriander, black pepper and parsley in a bowl. Rub the flesh side of the mackerel fillets with the olive oil, press over the spice mix and set to one side.

For the lentils, heat the sunflower oil in a large frying pan, add the onion and gently fry for 5 minutes. Add the garlic and garam masala and cook for a further minute. Add the lentils and stock to the pan and bring to the boil, then reduce the heat and simmer for 15–20 minutes or until the lentils are just tender.

To make the relish, simply mix all the ingredients together and season to taste with salt and pepper. Set to one side.

Heat a griddle pan, add the mackerel skin side down and cook over a medium-high heat for 2–3 minutes, then turn over and cook for 1–2 minutes on the other side until just cooked through.

To serve, stir the spinach into the lentils and spoon on to 4 warmed serving plates. Top each serving with 2 mackerel fillets and serve at once with the relish.

Don't be put off by the amount of garlic used here: because it is baked in its skin, it becomes deliciously sweet. Chicken thighs are juicy and full of flavour, but it's best to use skinless ones, as it keeps the sauce grease free.

Garlic & Thyme Chicken with Cannellini & Potato Mash

SERVES 4

4 tablespoons olive or rapeseed oil

8 large skinless chicken thighs

150ml (¼ pint) chicken stock

250ml (8fl oz) red wine

1 whole garlic bulb, separated into cloves but kept unpeeled

1 small bunch of thyme, broken into sprigs

1 large bay leaf

1 orange, halved

875g (1¾lb) floury white potatoes, peeled and cut into even-sized chunks

420g (14oz) can cannellini beans, drained and rinsed

4 tablespoons dairy-free milk

2 tablespoons chopped flat leaf parsley

4 tablespoons balsamic vinegar

pinch of sugar

salt and pepper

Preheat the oven to 190°C/fan 170°C/375°F/Gas Mark 5.

Place a medium-sized, heavy roasting tin on the hob over a medium heat, add half the oil and lay in the chicken thighs. Season with a little salt and lots of pepper. Fry the chicken thighs for a few minutes until beginning to colour. Meanwhile, mix together the stock and red wine in a jug.

Add the garlic cloves, thyme sprigs and the bay leaf to the roasting tin. Squeeze over the juice from the orange halves and toss in the squeezed halves. Pour in one-third of the wine and stock mixture and toss together well.

Bake the chicken pieces for about 30 minutes, turning over halfway through cooking, until cooked through – the juices should run clear when pierced through the thickest part with the tip of a knife.

Meanwhile, cook the potatoes in a saucepan of boiling water for 20–25 minutes until tender. Drain and return to the pan. Add the cannellini beans, milk and remaining oil and mash together. Stir in the parsley and season well with salt and pepper. Keep warm.

Place the chicken thighs in a serving dish along with half the garlic cloves, the orange halves and bay. Set to one side and keep warm. Squeeze the pulp from the remaining garlic cloves into the roasting tin. Place the tin on the hob over a medium heat, add the balsamic vinegar, remaining wine and stock mixture and the sugar and bring to the boil. Use a wooden spoon to scrape up the sediment from the base of the tin and mash in the garlic pulp. Simmer over a high heat for about 4 minutes or until syrupy. Season to taste with salt and pepper.

Pour the sauce over the chicken and serve with the cannellini and potato mash, along with lightly dressed baby spinach leaves.

This is a modern, speedy version of a classic French dish. The chorizo crumbs really give the chicken some oomph – you could use salami or black pudding in the crumb mixture instead. The creamy apple cassoulet is also great served with sausages or pork chops, or as a side dish with roast chicken.

Chorizo-crusted Chicken with Apple & Sage Cassoulet

SERVES 4

4 small boneless, skinless chicken breasts

125g (4oz) sliced cured chorizo sausage, very roughly chopped

225g (7½oz) dairy-free coarse fresh white breadcrumbs

2 free-range eggs, beaten

about 5 tablespoons olive or rapeseed oil

CASSOULET

3 dessert apples, quartered, cored and roughly chopped

2 red onions, finely chopped

400g (13oz) can cannellini beans, drained and rinsed

200ml (7fl oz) medium cider

200ml (7fl oz) chicken stock

2 teaspoons Dijon mustard

4 tablespoons dairy-free single cream

1 tablespoon chopped sage

1 tablespoon chopped parsley

salt and pepper

Preheat the oven to 160°C/fan 150°C/325°F/Gas Mark 3.

Place a chicken breast between 2 sheets of clingfilm and gently bat out with a rolling pin until almost doubled in size. Repeat with the remaining chicken breasts.

Place the chorizo in a food processor and pulse until finely chopped. Add the breadcrumbs and pulse until well mixed. Tip out on to a large plate.

Dip the chicken breasts in the beaten egg in a bowl and then coat with the chorizo crumbs.

Heat 2 tablespoons of the oil in a large, nonstick frying pan, add 2 chicken breasts and cook for about 3–4 minutes on each side or until golden and completely cooked through. Remove from the pan and keep warm in the oven. Repeat with the remaining chicken breasts.

To make the cassoulet, return the pan to the heat, add the remaining oil, the apples and onions and cook for over a medium heat for 5 minutes.

Add the beans, cider and stock and bring to the boil. Reduce the heat and simmer briskly until reduced by half.

Stir in the mustard, dairy-free cream and herbs, and season to taste with salt and pepper.

Spoon the cassoulet into 4 warmed serving dishes. Cut each chicken breast into 3 thick slices and place on top. Serve straight away.

A tortilla with a twist – tortillas sandwiched together with a bean, chicken and cheese filling, and cooked until melting in the middle and golden on the outside.

Smoky Quesadilla Melts with Chicken, Coriander & Avocado

SERVES 4

8 flour tortillas

400g (13oz) can mixed beans, drained, rinsed and patted dry

1 bunch of spring onions, finely chopped

5 tablespoons good-quality shop-bought mayonnaise or Smoked Garlic & Chive Mayo (see page 185)

1 tablespoon wholegrain mustard

250g (8oz) cooked chicken breast, skinned and thinly sliced

290g (9½oz) jar chargrilled peppers in oil, drained and cut into chunky slices (or you could use the Sweet Pepper Chutney on page 181)

1 bunch of coriander leaves, roughly chopped

1 large mild red chilli, finely chopped

1 large ripe avocado, halved, stoned, peeled and sliced

100g (3½oz) smoked cheddar-style soya cheese, finely grated

4 tablespoons olive oil

1 lime, cut into wedges

pepper

Place 4 of the tortillas on a work surface.

Gently mix together the beans, spring onions, mayonnaise and mustard in a bowl. Season well with pepper and spread the mixture evenly over the tortillas.

Arrange the chicken and peppers over the top and scatter over the coriander and chilli. Top with the avocado slices and finally scatter over the cheese.

Top each with one of the remaining flour tortillas and press down well to sandwich together.

Heat a medium-sized, nonstick frying pan and add 1 tablespoon of the oil. Using a large fish slice, carefully lift and place a filled tortilla in the hot pan. Place a medium-sized plate on the top and gently push down.

Cook over a medium heat for about 4–5 minutes, then remove the plate and quickly and carefully turn the quesadilla over – don't worry if a little filing comes out; just push it back in! Cook for a further 3–4 minutes until dark golden and heated through. Remove from the pan and keep warm in a low oven while you repeat with the remaining quesadillas, using the remaining oil.

Cut each quesadilla into 4 wedges and pile on a serving board. Serve with the lime wedges.

Succulent sesame chicken with a creamy hummus sauce – a marriage made in heaven! This fast marinade is also great with turkey and pork. Shop-bought hummus works well when time is short, but if you fancy it, try using the homemade variety on page 60.

Sesame Chicken Lickin'

SERVES 4

3 large boneless, skinless chicken breasts, about 175g (6oz) each, cut into finger strips

juice of 1 lemon

2 tablespoons olive oil

2 tablespoons wholegrain mustard

1 garlic clove, crushed

2 tablespoons clear honey

3 tablespoons sesame seeds

½ cucumber, peeled, deseeded and cut into small chunks

1 Cos lettuce, torn into bite-sized pieces

2 large carrots, peeled and then peeled into ribbons with a vegetable peeler

salt and pepper

SAUCE

200g (7oz) tub shop-bought hummus

3 tablespoons dairy-free natural yogurt

squeeze of lemon juice, to taste

pepper

4 pitta breads, to serve

Toss the chicken with the lemon juice, 1 tablespoon of the oil, the mustard, garlic and honey in a bowl. Season well with salt and pepper. Cover the bowl with clingfilm and set to one side for 10 minutes.

Heat the remaining oil in a large, nonstick wok or frying pan until hot. Add the chicken to the pan, reserving the marinade, and stir-fry for 4 minutes. Sprinkle over the sesame seeds and cook for a further 3–4 minutes until the seeds are golden and the chicken is just cooked through.

Pour in the marinade, bring to the boil and swirl the pan well until the chicken is sticky.

Meanwhile, mix together the hummus and yogurt in a bowl. Season to taste with lemon juice and pepper.

To serve, toast the pitta breads. Meanwhile, toss the salad ingredients together in a bowl. Divide the salad among 4 serving bowls and top each with the hot sesame chicken. Top with a dollop of the hummus sauce and serve with the toasted pittas.

This is a lovely curry and a perfect family choice, as it's creamy and very mildly spiced. It can be served with rice, but I usually serve it with this Tomato & Chilli Relish to cut through the richness. Homemade Socca bread (see page 139) and chapatis or crispy poppadums are also good accompaniments.

Creamy Chicken Curry

SERVES 4

1 tablespoon coconut oil

1 onion, finely sliced

1 large garlic clove, crushed

3 teaspoons ground turmeric

2 teaspoons ground coriander

1 teaspoon ground cumin

1 small cinnamon stick

2 bay leaves

3 tablespoons unsweetened desiccated coconut

3 large boneless, skinless chicken breasts, about 175g (6oz) each, cut into 5-cm (2-inch) chunks

425ml (14½fl oz) chicken stock

250ml (8fl oz) coconut cream

100g (3½oz) spinach leaves, shredded

salt and pepper

TOMATO & CHILLI RELISH

200g (7oz) baby plum tomatoes, quartered

2 red chillies, deseeded and finely chopped

pinch of sugar

1 tablespoon rapeseed oil

squeeze of lemon juice

Heat the coconut oil in nonstick saucepan, add the onion and cook gently for 10 minutes until softened. Stir in the garlic and cook for a further minute.

Add the spices and bay leaves and cook for 1 minute.

Stir in the coconut and cook for 1 minute until toasted.

Add the chicken, toss in the spice mix and cook for 1 minute.

Pour in the stock and coconut cream and bring to the boil, then reduce the heat and simmer gently for 20 minutes.

To make the relish, simply mix all the ingredients together in a bowl, season to taste with salt and pepper and spoon into a serving dish.

Add the spinach to the curry and cook for 1 minute. Season to taste with salt and pepper.

Serve the curry with the relish.

The new additions of fresh spinach and nutmeg really give this rich favourite a lighter, contemporary taste. If you fancy a fishy version simply toss through smoked salmon strips with the spinach at the end, leaving out the pancetta.

Spaghetti alla Carbonara

SERVES 4

350g (11½oz) dried spaghetti

2 tablespoons olive oil

125g (4oz) diced pancetta

2 large garlic cloves, crushed

3 large free-range eggs

85g (3¼oz) dairy-free Cheddar-style cheese, finely grated

50g (2oz) spinach, finely shredded

freshly grated nutmeg, to taste

salt and pepper

Place a large saucepan of water on to boil and stir in a good pinch of salt. Add the spaghetti and cook for about 10 minutes or until al dente.

Meanwhile, heat the oil in a large frying pan, add the pancetta and fry for 4–5 minutes until golden and crisp. Remove from the heat and stir in the garlic.

Beat the eggs together with the cheese in a bowl and season well with salt and pepper.

Drain the pasta, reserving some of the cooking liquid. Tip the pasta into the frying pan with the pancetta and garlic, then add 2 tablespoons of the reserved cooking liquid.

Place the pan over a medium heat and pour in the egg mixture. Using 2 wooden spoons, toss the spaghetti so that it mixes with the egg mixture and all the spaghetti is coated. Heat through until thickened, taking care not to overcook it or you will end up with scrambled egg!

At the last moment, stir through the spinach and season with plenty of black pepper and nutmeg. Serve straight away.

I'm very fussy about my pizza – making your own pizza bases really is worth the effort, and this dough is easy to prepare. I have suggested some more pizza toppings below, but feel free to experiment. Enjoy!

Pizza Pizza Pizza

MAKES 3 LARGE PIZZAS
(EACH PIZZA SERVES 2)

625g (1¼lb) cherry tomatoes, quartered

2 garlic cloves, crushed

4 tablespoons sun-dried tomato paste

3 tablespoons olive oil

DOUGH

680g (1lb 6oz) strong white flour, plus extra for dusting

1 teaspoon salt

2 x 7g (¼oz) sachets fast-action dried yeast

about 300ml (½ pint) warm water

4 tablespoons olive oil, plus extra for oiling

CLASSIC TOPPING

(Makes enough for 1 pizza)

4–5 tablespoons Classic Pesto (see page 184)

30g (1oz) rocket leaves

50g (2oz) thinly sliced salami, torn into strips

extra virgin olive oil, for drizzling

pepper

To make the pizza dough, sift the flour into a large bowl and then stir in the salt and yeast. Make a well in the centre of the flour mixture and pour in the measurement water and oil. Using a flat-bladed knife, draw the mixture in from the sides to form a soft, wet dough.

Knead the dough on a lightly floured surface for 10 minutes until smooth and elastic. Place the dough in a lightly oiled large bowl, cover with clingfilm and leave to rise in a warm place for about 1 hour or until doubled in size.

Preheat the oven to 210°C/fan 190°C/425°F/Gas Mark 7. Tip the risen dough out on to a lightly floured surface and knock back with a firm kneading. Divide the dough into 3 and roll each piece on a floured surface into a round measuring about 30cm (12 inches). Place on lightly floured baking sheets or pizza stones.

Toss the tomato quarters with the garlic and sun-dried tomato paste in a bowl and season well with salt and pepper. Divide the tomato mixture among the 3 pizza bases, pressing it down gently. Bake for about 20 minutes or until the pizza is crisp and the tomatoes have slightly caramelized.

To serve, finish each pizza with your chosen toppings, drizzle over a little olive oil and season with pepper.

Italiano Topping

Top with 175g (6oz) drained antipasti roasted peppers in oil, 100g (3½oz) pitted olives and a handful of basil leaves. Finish with olive oil.

Tropical Topping

Scatter over ¼ diced pineapple and 4 tablespoons drained canned sweetcorn, then crumble over 4 crisply grilled bacon rashers.

Any excuse for a quiche! I love to top mine with rocket leaves. My other favourite fillers are roasted peppers and pine nuts with my Classic Pesto (see page 184) spread on the base of the pastry case.

Classic Quiche

SERVES 6

PASTRY

275g (9oz) plain flour, plus extra for dusting

pinch of salt

140g (4½oz) dairy-free spread

1 egg, beaten

2–3 tablespoons cold water

FILLING

3 tablespoons wholegrain mustard

100g (3½oz) antipasti tomatoes in oil, drained and chopped

200g (7oz) smoked ham, cut into strips

100g (3½oz) dairy-free Cheddar-style cheese, finely grated

2 free-range eggs

2 free-range egg yolks

250ml (8fl oz) dairy-free single cream

250ml (8fl oz) oat or soya milk

1 small bunch of chives, chopped

SALAD TOPPING

1 tablespoon extra virgin olive oil

1 tablespoon balsamic vinegar

50g (2oz) rocket leaves

Preheat the oven to 190°C/fan 170°C/375°F/Gas Mark 5.

Sift the flour into a bowl and stir in the salt. Add the spread in small pieces and lightly rub in with your fingertips until the mixture resembles fine breadcrumbs. Alternatively, place the ingredients in a food processor and whizz together. Gently mix in the egg and enough of the water to bind the pastry dough together. Pat into a rough, flat disc, wrap in clingfilm and chill in the refrigerator for 30 minutes.

Roll out the pastry gently on a lightly floured surface and use to line a 28-cm (11-inch) loose-bottomed flan tin. Cover with clingfilm and chill in the refrigerator for 15 minutes.

Line the pastry case with baking parchment and half-fill with baking beans. Bake blind for 10 minutes. Remove the pastry case from the oven and lift out the paper and beans. Return to the oven for a further 5 minutes. Remove from oven and increase the temperature to 200°C/fan 180°C/400°F/Gas Mark 6.

For the filling, spoon the mustard over the base of the pastry case, then scatter over the tomatoes, ham and half the cheese. Beat together the eggs, egg yolks, cream and milk in a bowl. Season well with salt and pepper and stir in the chives. Pour the mixture carefully into the pastry case and scatter over the remaining cheese.

Bake for 25–30 minutes until the filling is golden and just set.

Remove the quiche from oven and leave to cool for 10 minutes, then transfer to a serving plate.

Mix together the olive oil and balsamic vinegar in a large bowl. Season to taste with salt and pepper. Toss in the rocket leaves and pile in the centre of the quiche just before serving.

This dish is often spoilt by soggy veg, but by roasting the cauliflower and broccoli, you not only intensify the flavour but get firmer florets! It's most important to rinse the veggies well, as the water clinging to them will help in the cooking.

Roasted Cauliflower & Broccoli Mornay with a Chorizo Crumb

SERVES 4

4 tablespoons olive oil

1 cauliflower, broken into small–medium-sized florets

225g (7½oz) broccoli, broken into medium–large florets

30g (1oz) plain flour

600ml (1 pint) soya milk

85g (3¼oz) dairy-free strong Cheddar-style cheese, finely grated

2 tablespoons dairy-free single cream

squeeze of lemon juice

100g (3½oz) sliced cured chorizo sausage, roughly chopped

50g (2oz) dairy-free fresh white breadcrumbs

salt and pepper

Preheat the oven to 200°C/fan 180°C/400°F/Gas Mark 6.

Spoon half the oil into a shallow, flameproof, ovenproof dish and place over a medium heat.

Meanwhile, rinse the vegetable florets under cold water. Add the wet florets to the hot pan. Toss together and season well with salt and pepper. Rinse a round of greaseproof paper the size of the pan under cold water and place over the vegetables. Cover with a tight-fitting lid or foil, place in the oven and bake for about 18–20 minutes or until the veg are just tender.

While the veg are baking, heat the remaining oil in a saucepan, add the flour and cook over a medium heat for 30 seconds. Remove from the heat and add all the soya milk. Whisk well until all the lumps have gone, then return to heat and bring to the boil, stirring constantly. Simmer for 4–5 minutes until thickish and smooth. Add the dairy-free cheese and cream, remove from the heat and stir until melted. Stir in the lemon juice and season to taste with salt and pepper.

For the crumbs, add the chorizo to a food processor and whizz until finely chopped. Place a medium-sized frying pan over a medium heat, add the chopped chorizo and fry for 3–4 minutes until golden. Add the breadcrumbs to the pan and fry for 2–3 minutes. Set to one side.

Remove the vegetable florets from the oven, pour over the mornay sauce and sprinkle over the chorizo crumbs. Return to the oven for 12–15 minutes until bubbling and golden. Serve at once.

Homemade lasagne without too much faff! This classic favourite is enhanced with red wine, field mushrooms and a thin layer of prosciutto ham, all topped off with a thick layer of no-cook creamy cheese sauce. Make sure you choose dried lasagne sheets that need no pre-cooking, which are widely available and mostly dairy free.

Luxury Beef & Prosciutto Lasagne with a Cheesy Nutmeg Sauce

SERVES 6

2 tablespoons olive oil

1 large onion, chopped

2 garlic cloves, crushed

250g (8oz) field mushrooms, peeled and chopped

400g (13oz) good-quality lean minced beef

150ml (¼ pint) red wine

500g (1lb) carton tomato passata (sieved tomatoes)

400g (13oz) can chopped tomatoes

1 tablespoon thyme leaves

2 bay leaves

250g (8oz) dairy-free cream cheese

150ml (¼ pint) dairy-free single cream

75g (3oz) dairy-free strong Cheddar-style cheese, finely grated

good grating of nutmeg

6 no-precook sheets of dried lasagne

4 slices of prosciutto ham

salt and pepper

Preheat the oven to 200°C/fan 180°C/400°F/Gas Mark 6.

Heat the oil a large, nonstick saucepan until hot. Stir in the onion and cook over a medium heat for 4–5 minutes or until softened. Stir in the garlic, add the mushrooms and cook over a high heat until all the liquid has evaporated.

Stir in the minced beef and fry, breaking up with a wooden spoon, for 4–5 minutes until browned. Add the red wine, passata, canned tomatoes and herbs and season well with salt and pepper. Simmer for 25–30 minutes.

Meanwhile, for the cheese sauce, stir together the cream cheese, cream and 60g (2¼oz) of the grated cheese and season with the nutmeg and salt and pepper.

Spoon half the meat sauce into a nonstick roasting tin or shallow ovenproof dish about 20cm x 25cm (8 inches x 10 inches). Top with 3 lasagne sheets and then with the remaining meat sauce and another 3 lasagne sheets. Lay over the prosciutto ham, pour over the cheese sauce and scatter over the remaining grated cheese.

Bake for about 30–35 minutes until bubbling and golden.

The muscovado and vinegar in these thick, tomato-coated beans create a wonderful sweet and sour flavour. The dumplings are quick to whip up and make a tasty and lighter alternative to the classic suet dumpling.

Boston Bean Bake Topped with Olive Oil & Herb Dumplings

SERVES 4

1 tablespoon olive oil, plus extra for drizzling

1 large onion, chopped

1 large garlic clove, crushed

410g (13½oz) can borlotti beans, drained and rinsed

410g (13½oz) can haricot beans, drained and rinsed

1 tablespoon Dijon mustard

2 tablespoons light muscovado sugar

2 tablespoons white wine vinegar

500g (1lb) carton passata (sieved tomatoes)

150ml (¼ pint) water

12 chipolatas

DUMPLINGS

225g (7½oz) self-raising flour

3 tablespoons chopped parsley

1 tablespoon chopped sage

1 tablespoon thyme leaves

2 tablespoons olive oil

150ml (¼ pint) oat or other dairy-free milk

salt and pepper

Preheat the oven to 200°C/fan 180°C/400°F/Gas Mark 6.

Heat the oil in a flameproof casserole dish or other ovenproof pan, add the onion and fry for 5–6 minutes until golden and softened. Add the garlic and fry for 1 minute.

Stir in the beans, mustard, sugar and vinegar. Bring to the boil, then reduce the heat and simmer for 2 minutes. Add the passata and measurement water and return to the boil, then gently simmer for 15 minutes.

Meanwhile, place the chipolatas in a small roasting tin and drizzle with a little olive oil. Cook in the oven for 20 minutes.

When the beans and chipolatas are near the end of their cooking time, make the dumplings. Place the flour in a bowl and season well with salt and pepper. Stir in the herbs. Add the oil and milk and stir lightly with a fork to make a soft dough. With floured hands, roll into 12 dumplings.

Remove the chipolatas from the oven and place in the pan with the beans. Place the dumplings on top and bake in the oven for 25 minutes or until the dumplings are golden and just firm.

These meatballs are soft, succulent and incredibly moreish. They're also very versatile: they can be served with spaghetti, stuffed in a baked potato or simply served with a green salad and some bread to mop up the sauce. For a supper party sensation, serve on Creamy Mustard Mash (see page 73) with Cranberry, Red Cabbage & Juniper Jam (see page 180).

Soft Beef Kofta Meatballs in Sticky Glaze

SERVES 4

2 tablespoons olive oil

1 onion, finely chopped

2 garlic cloves, crushed

750g (1½lb) lean minced beef

150g (5oz) dairy-free fresh white breadcrumbs

1 medium egg, beaten

125ml (4fl oz) dairy-free single cream

good grating of nutmeg

salt and pepper

GLAZE

2 tablespoons plain flour

300ml (½ pint) red wine

600ml (1 pint) chicken stock

2 tablespoons syrupy balsamic vinegar

pinch of sugar

Preheat the oven to 200°C/fan 180°C/400°F/Gas Mark 6.

Heat half the oil in a frying or sauté pan, add the onion and cook gently for 5 minutes until softened. Add the garlic and cook for 2 minutes. Remove from heat, transfer to a large bowl and allow to cool.

Add the minced beef to the cooled onion with the remaining ingredients, season with salt and pepper and mix really well – it's best to use your hands here.

To check that the seasoning is right, fry a little of the mixture in a pan until cooked through and taste, correcting the seasoning if necessary.

Divide the mixture into 24 equal-sized balls and place in a roasting tin. Drizzle over the remaining oil and shake to coat in the oil. Roast for 30 minutes, giving the meatballs a shake now and then. Remove from oven, transfer the meatballs to a serving plate and keep warm in the oven on low.

To make the glaze, drain the oil from the roasting tin, reserving 1 tablespoon. Pour the tablespoon of oil back into the roasting tin and place over a medium heat on the hob. Sprinkle over the flour, stir well with a wooden spoon and cook out for 2 minutes, scraping all the sediment from the bottom of the pan (this will give it flavour and colour).

Add the red wine, stock and balsamic vinegar and simmer over a high heat for 5–10 minutes or until syrupy. Season to taste with salt and pepper and add the sugar.

Strain the sauce over the meatballs and serve.

Madras curry paste and peanut butter make an excellent base for a hot, nutty sauce. Here they are tossed with sesame noodles, stir-fried vegetables and sizzling beef to make a speedy supper.

Nutty Noodles with Wilted Greens & Sticky Beef

SERVES 4

400g (13oz) flash-fry steak, cut into finger strips

4 tablespoons syrupy teriyaki sauce

1 teaspoon chilli flakes

375g (12oz) medium egg noodles

1 tablespoon sesame oil

1 tablespoon groundnut oil

2 large carrots, peeled and cut into strips

175g (6oz) cavolo nero or spring greens, finely shredded

150g (5oz) podded fresh peas

1 small bunch of coriander, roughly chopped

SAUCE

2 tablespoons Madras curry paste

3 tablespoons crunchy peanut butter (see page 178 for homemade)

1 tablespoon dark soy sauce

300ml (½ pint) coconut milk

pepper

Place the beef strips in a bowl with the teriyaki sauce and chilli flakes. Mix well to combine and set to one side.

Cook the noodles according to the packet instructions, then drain, toss with the sesame oil and set to one side.

Meanwhile, to make the sauce, heat a small saucepan, add the curry paste and cook over a medium heat, stirring constantly, for 1 minute. Add the peanut butter, soy sauce and coconut milk and stir well, then season with pepper. Bring to the boil, then reduce the heat and simmer for 2 minutes.

Heat the groundnut oil in a large wok or nonstick frying pan over a high heat. Add the beef with all the marinade and stir-fry for 2 minutes. Add the carrots, cavolo nero or spring greens and peas and stir-fry for a further 2 minutes.

Arrange the sesame noodles in 4 warmed serving bowls and divide the stir-fried beef and vegetables on top. Spoon over the peanut sauce and finish with the chopped coriander. Serve straight away.

This one-pan dish uses pork tenderloin, as it's lean and tender and great cut into small medallion steaks. It needs to be pan-fried gently to allow all the sugars from the prunes to become sticky and caramelize and make a delicious creamy pan sauce.

Pork & Prune Medallions with Creamy Cider & Mustard Sauce

SERVES 4

450g (1lb) pork fillet

12 large ready-to-eat prunes, halved

24 small sage leaves

4 tablespoons plain flour

2 tablespoons olive oil

250ml (8fl oz) cider

2–3 teaspoons wholegrain mustard

25g (1oz) dairy-free Cheddar-style cheese, finely grated

5 tablespoons dairy-free single cream

salt and pepper

Trim and slice the pork fillet on a slant into 12 pieces. Using the palm of your hand, gently flatten the pieces of pork into medallion shapes.

Using a small, sharp knife, cut 2 slits into each medallion. Push half a prune and 2 sage leaves into each cut. Season with pepper.

Place the flour on a plate and season well with salt and pepper. Dust each pork medallion in a little of the seasoned flour.

Heat half the oil in a nonstick frying pan, lay in 6 stuffed pork medallions and cook over a medium heat for 4–5 minutes on each side until golden and cooked through. Remove and keep warm. Repeat with the remaining pork medallions.

Splash in the cider and simmer until reduced by half, then stir in the mustard, cheese and the cream. Season to taste with salt and pepper.

Serve the pork medallions with the sauce, fine green beans and roasted new potatoes.

Weekend
Delights

A stylish, no-cook mezze dish, which is great served with homemade focaccia (see page 138) or dairy-free sourdough. Charentais is the best melon to use, as it's so sweet, juicy and colourful. Simply take to the table and let everyone tuck in!

Melon, Ham & Pine Nut Salad

SERVES 4

3 large orange peppers, halved, cored and deseeded

3 tablespoons extra virgin olive oil

1 small ripe Charentais melon

100g (3½oz) rocket leaves

125g (4oz) slices of air-cured ham

50g (2oz) pine nuts, toasted

1 tablespoon good-quality balsamic vinegar

pepper

Preheat the oven to 210°C/fan 190°C/425°F/Gas Mark 7. Place the peppers in a roasting tin and drizzle over 1 tablespoon of the olive oil. Roast for 20–25 minutes. Remove from the oven and set to one side to cool.

Cut the melon in half and scoop out the seeds. Cut each half into 4 wedges.

Arrange the melon on a large board and season with pepper. Trickle over the remaining olive oil, then scatter over the rocket, roasted peppers, ham and pine nuts. Finish with a generous grinding of black pepper and drizzle over the balsamic vinegar.

The classic way to cook asparagus is to steam it, but I rarely do that now, as I love to roast it with just a drizzle of olive oil and a splash of water. It's so easy this way and I think much more delicious.

Asparagus with Watercress & Candied Walnut Salad

SERVES 4

100g (3½oz) shelled walnuts

3 tablespoons olive oil

1½ tablespoons caster sugar

pinch of salt

2 bunches of asparagus, trimmed

1 bunch of watercress, leaves picked

1 tablespoon balsamic vinegar

salt and pepper

4 tablespoons Smoked Garlic & Chive Mayo (see page 185), to serve

Preheat the oven to 200°C/fan 180°C/400°F/Gas Mark 6.

To make the candied walnuts, toss the nuts in 1 tablespoon of the oil in a bowl and sprinkle over the sugar and salt. Toss well to coat and transfer to a baking sheet. Place in the oven for 5 minutes. Remove from the oven and give the nuts a shake, then return to the oven for 2–3 minutes or until golden. Set to one side until needed.

Wash the asparagus and place wet in a roasting tin, drizzle with 1 tablespoon of olive oil and season well with salt and pepper. Roast for 6–8 minutes or until just tender.

Place the watercress in a bowl and lightly dress with the balsamic vinegar and the remaining olive oil. Toss in the warm walnuts.

Divide the salad among 4 serving plates and top each with the asparagus. Serve with a dollop of Smoked Garlic & Chive Mayo.

This is a modern take on a retro starter. Sadly, it could sometimes be ruined by overcooked eggs – the secret is to cook them so that the yolks are just set. Fold into creamy, smoky mayo and layer up with the piquant tapenade, then finish with a top hat of mustard and cress. Serve with plenty of toast and a glass of fizz, but it's also really good just used as a filling to make a tasty sarni.

Vintage Egg Mayo with Tapenade & Cress

SERVES 4

6 free-range eggs

4 tablespoons Smoked Garlic & Chive Mayo (see page 185)

3 anchovy fillets, drained

12 large good-quality black olives, pitted

2 tablespoons baby capers, drained

1 punnet mustard and cress

pepper

Place the eggs in a saucepan, cover with cold water and bring to the boil, then reduce the heat and simmer for 3½ minutes.

Immediately remove the eggs from pan and place in cold water to prevent further cooking. Carefully shell the eggs and roughly chop – not too finely.

Lightly mix the chopped eggs with the mayo and season to taste with pepper.

Finely chop the anchovies and olives and mix with the capers.

Carefully spoon half the egg mixture into 4 large shot glasses and divide half the anchovy mixture among them. Repeat with a further layer of each.

Finish with a mound of mustard and cress on each and serve with slices of toasted dairy-free sourdough or rye bread, or Caramelized Onion & Spelt Flatbread (see page 136).

This is a real showstopper that doesn't require much effort at all. Serve rustic style on a wooden board or much smaller as a canapé. It's perfect for alfresco entertaining – you could even toast the bread on the barbecue and assemble the dish in front of your guests. The oranges and shallots cut through the richness of the smoked trout and avocado.

Smoked Trout Bruschetta with Orange & Dill Relish

SERVES 4–6

150ml (¼ pint) dairy-free single cream

4–5 teaspoons dairy-free horseradish sauce

squeeze of lemon juice

400g (13oz) skinless smoked trout fillets

1 dairy-free ciabatta-style rustic loaf

2 tablespoons olive oil

pepper

ORANGE & DILL RELISH

2 ripe avocados, halved and stoned

2 oranges, peeled and white pith removed

2 large shallots, finely sliced

2 tablespoons extra virgin olive oil

1 small bunch of dill, plus extra sprigs to garnish

salt and pepper

Preheat the oven to 200°C/fan 180°C/400°F/Gas Mark 6.

Mix together the cream, horseradish and lemon juice in a large bowl. Season with pepper. Break the trout into large flakes and gently fold into the horseradish mixture. Set to one side.

Cut the loaf in half horizontally and lay both halves on a baking sheet. Drizzle over the olive oil and bake in the oven for 12 minutes until golden and toasty.

Meanwhile, to make the relish, spoon the avocado flesh out of the shells in dollops. Segment the oranges by cutting between the membranes, catching the juice from one orange and squeezing out any juices remaining in the membrane.

Gently mix together the avocado, orange segments and reserved juice, shallots, extra virgin olive oil and dill. Season to taste with salt and pepper.

To serve, arrange the loaf halves on a large wooden board. Cut each half into 5. Top each ciabatta slice with the trout mixture. Grind over a little more black pepper and top with the relish and extra dill sprigs. Take to the table and serve.

This makes a stylish, sophisticated starter for six, or a lunch or supper for four. Creamy spinach, smoked salmon and horseradish make a wonderful flavour combination. If you love poached eggs, try them here – they are a great addition to this dish. Use cold-smoked salmon if you can't get hold of hot-smoked fillets.

Hot-smoked Salmon Horseradish Crème with Fresh Spinach Sauce

SERVES 4–6

30ml (1fl oz) olive oil

2 onions, chopped

2 garlic cloves, crushed

2 potatoes, peeled, halved and thinly sliced (approximately 225g/7½oz prepared weight)

1 litre (1¾ pints) vegetable stock

235g (7½oz) bag ready-washed spinach leaves

generous grating of nutmeg

6 x 85g (3¼oz) pieces of hot-smoked cured salmon fillets

salt and pepper

TO SERVE

3 tablespoons dairy-free single cream

2–3 teaspoons dairy-free hot horseradish sauce

handful of spinach leaves, finely shredded

Preheat the oven to 200°C/fan 180°C/400°F/Gas Mark 6.

Heat the oil in a large saucepan and add the onions, then cover with a lid and cook over a medium heat, stirring occasionally, for 10 minutes until softened. Add the garlic and potatoes and cook for a further 5 minutes.

Add the stock to the pan and bring to the boil, then cover, reduce the heat and simmer for 10 minutes. Add the whole spinach leaves, nutmeg and salt and pepper to taste, then cook for a minute until the spinach has wilted.

Remove the pan from the heat and allow to cool a little. Transfer the sauce to a blender or food processor and blend until smooth. Return to a clean saucepan, reheat and check the seasoning.

Place the salmon pieces on a baking sheet and warm through for about 5–6 minutes.

Meanwhile, mix together the cream and horseradish and season to taste with salt and pepper.

Remove the skin from the hot salmon. To serve, simply ladle the sauce into 6 warmed shallow bowls and top with the salmon pieces, horseradish cream and shredded raw spinach.

Caramelized pears are given an unusual sweet and sour hit here. The best pears to use are Conference, and they don't have to be ripe. They are served here starter style, warm with serrano ham and rocket along with crusty bread, but they're equally great served as an accompaniment to roast pork, baked ham or roast duck.

Roasted Salt & Pepper Pears & Serrano Platter

SERVES 4

6 ripe Conference pears

2 teaspoons cracked black pepper

6 teaspoons caster sugar

1 teaspoon sea salt

5 tablespoons cider vinegar

2 tablespoons olive oil

TO SERVE

2 handfuls of dressed rocket leaves

125g (4oz) serrano ham, pastrami or salt beef

extra virgin olive oil, for drizzling

1 warm crusty loaf

Preheat the oven to 200°C/fan 180°C/400°F/Gas Mark 6.

Peel and halve the pears (keeping the stalks intact), then lay cut side up in a shallow, nonstick roasting tray.

Place the cracked pepper, sugar and salt in a small bowl and mix together well. Scatter over the pears. Drizzle over the vinegar, oil and 2 tablespoons water.

Roast for 25 minutes, then remove the tray from the oven, turn the pears over and drizzle over a further 3 tablespoons water. Return to the oven for 10–15 minutes until the pears are golden and just tender.

To serve, place the pears cut side up on a large platter or rustic board. Top with the dressed rocket, tear over the serrano ham, pastrami or salt beef and drizzle with a little olive oil. Take to the table with a basket of warm bread.

This fresh, fruity warm salad works perfectly with the rich, crispy duck breast. I was taught many years ago how to get a really crisp skin on duck breast without overcooking the meat. The duck is best served pink and the trick is to allow it to rest for at least 5 minutes before slicing and arranging on the salad.

Duck with Warm Pomegranate, Puy Lentil & Orange Salad

SERVES 4 AS A STARTER

2 small duck breasts, skin on

sea salt, for rubbing

50g (2oz) dried Puy lentils, washed and cooked according to the packet instructions

1 small red onion, finely sliced

1 garlic clove, crushed

3 tablespoons olive oil

seeds of 1 pomegranate

1 large orange, segmented and juice reserved

1 small bunch of flat leaf parsley, roughly torn

salt and pepper

Preheat the oven to 210°C/fan 190°C/425°F/Gas Mark 7.

Using a small knife, score the skin of the duck in a lattice fashion and rub each with a little sea salt.

Heat a large frying pan over a medium heat, add the breasts skin side down and cook for 4 minutes until really golden, then turn over and sear for a further 30 seconds.

Transfer the duck to a wire rack over a roasting tin, skin side up. Roast the duck for 6 minutes. Remove from the oven and allow to rest in a warm place for 10 minutes.

Meanwhile, mix together the remaining ingredients in a large bowl. Season to taste with salt and pepper.

To serve, arrange the salad on 4 serving plates. Slice the duck into thin slices and arrange on top of the salad. Serve straight away.

I just love this pie! The pastry is so easy to handle that it doesn't need to be chilled before rolling. The mound of potato and celeriac steams under the pastry crust. It needs at least an hour's cooking, depending on how thinly you slice your potatoes and celeriac, and the end result is crisp and delicious. If celeriac isn't in season, use all potato.

Potato & Celeriac Pie with Rapeseed Crust

SERVES 8

500g (1lb) white potatoes, peeled and cut into 5-mm (¼-inch) slices

1 celeriac, peeled and cut into 5-mm (¼-inch) slices

2 large shallots, finely chopped

2 garlic cloves, crushed

2 tablespoons rapeseed oil

1 small bunch of chives, chopped

1 quantity of Soured Cream & Tarragon Dressing (see page 183)

salt and pepper

PASTRY

575g (1lb 3oz) plain flour, plus extra for dusting

pinch of salt

200ml (7fl oz) rapeseed oil

150ml (¼ pint) cold water, plus extra if needed

beaten egg, to glaze

Place the potato and celeriac slices in a large bowl. Toss in the shallots, garlic, oil and chives and season really well with salt and pepper. Set to one side for 15 minutes.

Preheat the oven to 200°C/fan 180°C/400°F/Gas Mark 6. Line a baking sheet with baking parchment.

To make the pastry, sift the flour into a large bowl and stir in the salt. Mix the oil and measurement water together in a jug, then gently mix into the flour mixture to bind the pastry dough together. If too dry, add a little more water.

Roll out one-third of the pastry on a lightly floured surface into a 30-cm (12-inch) round and place on the lined baking sheet.

Pile on the potato and celeriac mixture, leaving a 2.5-cm (1-inch) border around the edge. Roll out the remaining pastry into a 35-cm (14-inch) round and carefully place over the top. Gently press down to seal the edges and roll the edges up to form a thick rim.

Brush the pie with the beaten egg to glaze and bake for 1¼ hours. If getting too dark, reduce the heat to 190°C/fan 170°C/375°F/Gas Mark 5 and cover with a sheet of foil.

Remove the pie from the oven and allow to cool for a few minutes. Using a serrated knife, carefully cut off the top of the pastry lid.

Spoon the soured cream dressing over the potatoes. Replace the pastry top and allow to stand for 5 minutes.

Transfer the pie to a serving board. Serve hot, warm or cold with baked ham, spiced beef, such as pastrami, or smoked salmon.

This special crab tart is superb with the soy–chilli dressing and sesame crust. If fresh crabmeat is tricky to find, you can use fresh cooked prawns or cooked crayfish tails instead.

Crab & Ginger Tart with Soy–chilli Dressing

SERVES 6 AS A MAIN COURSE
OR 12 AS A STARTER

10-cm (4-inch) piece of fresh root ginger, peeled and roughly chopped

1 large bunch of flat leaf parsley

2 tablespoons sunflower oil

350g (11½oz) fresh white crabmeat

2 free-range eggs

2 free-range egg yolks

grated rind of 1 unwaxed lime

325ml (11fl oz) dairy-free single cream

CRUST

300g (10oz) plain flour, plus extra for dusting

1 teaspoon sea salt

3 tablespoons sesame seeds

75ml (2½fl oz) extra virgin olive oil

about 75ml (2½fl oz) cold water

DRESSING

4 spring onions, finely chopped

juice of 1 lime

1 red chilli, finely chopped

3 tablespoons dark soy sauce

6 tablespoons sunflower oil

1 teaspoon caster sugar

1 tablespoon water

For the crust, mix together the flour, salt and sesame seeds in a large bowl. Stir in the oil and measurement water (you may need slightly less or slightly more water depending on your flour). Using your hands, bring the dough together and form into a flat disc.

Preheat the oven to 200°C/fan 180°C/400°F/Gas Mark 6.

Roll out the pastry gently on a lightly floured surface and use to line a 28-cm (11-inch) loose-bottomed flan tin. Cover with clingfilm and chill in the refrigerator for 15 minutes.

Line the tart case with baking parchment paper and half-fill with baking beans. Bake blind for 10–15 minutes. Remove the tart case from the oven and lift out the paper and beans. Return the tart case to the oven for a further 3–5 minutes until it is just cooked. Reduce the heat to 190°C/fan 170°C/375°F/Gas Mark 5.

Place the ginger, parsley and sunflower oil in a small food processor and blend together into a paste. Spread over the base of the tart case. Scatter the crabmeat over the top of the ginger paste.

Beat together the eggs, egg yolks, lime rind and cream in a bowl and season with salt and pepper. Pour into the tart case. Bake the tart for 30–35 minutes or until just set.

Meanwhile, whisk all the dressing ingredients together in a small bowl. Season to taste with salt and pepper.

Serve the tart warm with a drizzling of the soy–chilli dressing.

Named after the clay dish in which it's traditionally cooked, this dish is full of Moroccan flavours. It's all about the spices and the gentle cook, which keeps the chicken moist. You don't need a tagine to make this, just a decent casserole dish with a tight-fitting lid. I serve this with lentils and rice, but couscous can be served instead.

Chicken Tagine with Red Lentils & Rice

SERVES 4

2 tablespoons olive oil

8 skinless chicken thighs

1 garlic clove, crushed

1 tablespoon ground cumin

1 tablespoon coriander seeds, crushed

1 tablespoon sweet smoked paprika

1 onion, sliced

400g (13oz) can chopped tomatoes

400ml (14fl oz) vegetable stock

200ml (7fl oz) red wine

200g (7oz) dried apricots

1 cinnamon stick

2 tablespoons chopped mint

RED LENTILS & RICE

150g (5oz) red split lentils, washed

150g (5oz) basmati rice, washed

2 tablespoons olive oil

juice of ½ lemon, or to taste

Preheat oven to 180°C/fan 160°C/350°F/Gas Mark 4.

Rub 1 tablespoon of the olive oil into the chicken thighs. Mix together the garlic, cumin, coriander and paprika and rub over the chicken thighs on both sides.

Heat a large, nonstick frying pan, add the chicken thighs and cook over a medium heat for 5 minutes until golden on both sides. Remove from the pan and set to one side.

Add the remaining oil to the pan and cook the onion for 5 minutes or until softened. Stir in the tomatoes, stock, red wine, apricots and cinnamon stick and bring to the boil.

Pour the sauce into a casserole dish and place the chicken thighs and any juices on top. Cover with the lid, place in the oven and cook for 1½ hours.

After the tagine has been cooking for an hour, prepare the lentils and rice. Place the lentils in a pan, cover with plenty of cold water and bring to the boil. Reduce the heat and simmer for 15–20 minutes. Drain well.

Meanwhile, cook the basmati rice according to the packet instructions, then drain well if necessary.

Toss the cooked lentils and rice together in a bowl and add the olive oil and lemon juice to taste.

Scatter the mint over the chicken tagine and serve with the lentils and rice.

I love baked risotto because you get a combination of soft, creamy rice along with a crisp, baked rice topping. The saffron, orange and bay flavours infuse into the rice while the poussin roasts on top. I have tried this with small chickens and large chicken joints, but it doesn't work as well, so stick to poussin for the best results.

Saffron-baked Orange Poussin with Crispy-topped Risotto

SERVES 4

4 single-serve poussins

4 garlic cloves, crushed

4 bay leaves

1 small bunch of lemon thyme, bruised

3 small oranges, halved

150ml (¼ pint) white wine

4 tablespoons olive oil, plus extra for brushing

about 1 litre (1¾ pints) chicken stock

2 good pinches of saffron threads

2 large Spanish onions, sliced

450g (14½oz) risotto rice

salt and pepper

Place the poussins in a large glass or ceramic bowl and season well with salt and pepper. Rub over the garlic and sprinkle over the herbs. Squeeze over the juice from the orange halves and add the squeezed halves, then pour in the white wine and half the oil.

Cover the bowl with clingfilm and leave to marinate in the refrigerator for 2 hours, or even better overnight.

Preheat the oven to 200°C/fan 180°C/400°F/Gas Mark 6.

Heat the stock in a saucepan and add the saffron threads. Set to one side.

Heat the remaining oil in a paella pan or large, heavy roasting tin, add the onions and fry for 5 minutes or so until softened. Stir in the rice and cook for 1 minute.

Place the poussins breast side down on top of the rice and pour over the marinade juices and orange halves and 600ml (1 pint) of the stock. Bring to the boil, then cover with foil, transfer to the oven and cook for 25 minutes.

Remove the pan or tin from the oven, turn the poussins over and add the remaining stock. Brush the poussins with a little extra oil and season well with salt and pepper.

Return to the oven, uncovered, and cook for a further 30 minutes or until the poussins and rice are cooked. You may need to add extra stock during cooking.

This delicious roast bird is served with a rich wine ragout and a creamy cardamom bread sauce. If guinea fowl is not available, the dish also works really well with chicken. I love to serve this with roasted vegetables.

Roasted Guinea Fowl with Cardamom Bread Sauce

SERVES 4

600ml (1 pint) red wine

225g (7½oz) ready-to-eat prunes

1 guinea fowl, about 1.75kg (3½lb)

4 red onions, cut into 6 wedges

1 teaspoon caster sugar

1 small bunch of thyme

1 tablespoon olive oil

1 tablespoon balsamic syrup

7g (¼oz) bitter dark chocolate

salt and pepper

CARDAMOM BREAD SAUCE

1 large onion, cut into quarters

12 cardamom pods, lightly crushed

12 black peppercorns

about 300ml (½ pint) almond milk (see page 177 for homemade)

85g (3⅓oz) dairy-free fresh white breadcrumbs

4 tablespoons dairy-free single cream

salt and pepper

Pour the red wine into a bowl, add the prunes and leave to soak for about two hours, then drain.

Preheat the oven to 200°C/fan 180°C/400°F/Gas Mark 6.

Loosely tie the legs of the guinea fowl with kitchen string. Season well with salt and pepper and place in a large roasting tin. Arrange the red onions and prunes around the guinea fowl, pour over the wine, sprinkle over the sugar and top with the thyme. Drizzle over the oil.

Roast the bird for about 1¼ hours until it is dark golden brown and the juices run clear when the thickest part of the thigh is pierced with the tip of a knife. Baste frequently during the cooking time.

Meanwhile, to make the bread sauce, place the onion, cardamom, peppercorns and almond milk in a saucepan and leave to infuse for 30 minutes.

Place the pan over a low heat and gently bring to the boil. Remove from the heat and strain on to the breadcrumbs in a bowl. Beat in the cream and return to the cleaned saucepan. Season well with salt and pepper.

Remove the guinea fowl from the roasting tin and allow to rest in a warm place for 10 minutes while you finish the sauce.

Reheat the bread sauce, stirring constantly, but do not let it boil. If the sauce becomes too thick, add more milk to obtain a creamy consistency.

Place the roasting tin on the hob, add the balsamic syrup and reduce until syrupy. Stir in the chocolate and season to taste.

Carve the bird. Serve the guinea fowl with a spoonful of the onion, prunes and juices, and hand round a bowl of the bread sauce.

With this one-pot wonder, there is no need to seal the meat first or fry off the shallots. All you do is layer up the ingredients in the pan, place on a tight-fitting lid and cook in the oven for 4 hours. Incredibly the lamb caramelizes and everything is ready at the same time. I originally tried this with preserved lemons, but the end result was too overpowering, while the fresh lemons work superbly.

Slow-cooked Lamb with Lemon & Oregano

SERVES 4–6

2 tablespoons extra virgin olive oil

875g (1¾lb) waxy new potatoes, washed and thickly sliced

6 banana shallots, peeled but kept whole

1 whole garlic bulb, cut in half across the middle

4 good oregano sprigs

3 bay leaves

2 teaspoons sea salt

1 teaspoon cracked black pepper

about 1.75kg (3½lb) (unboned weight) shoulder of lamb, boned

2 small unwaxed lemons, cut into quarters

200ml (7fl oz) vegetable stock

salt and pepper

Preheat the oven to 160°C/fan 150°C/325°F/Gas Mark 3.

Pour the oil into a large ovenproof pan and add the potatoes, shallots, garlic, oregano, bay leaves, sea salt and cracked pepper.

Trim the lamb and cut into 8–10 large chunks. Place in a bowl, squeeze over the juice from the lemon quarters and season with salt and pepper.

Arrange the lamb and squeezed lemon quarters on top of the vegetables and pour over the stock. Cover with a tight-fitting lid and cook in the oven for 3½–4 hours until tender, basting the lamb with the juices occasionally.

To serve, spoon the lamb on to a large warmed platter, top with the potatoes, shallots, garlic and herbs and spoon over the juices. Serve with fine green beans and a simple watercress salad.

Crisp, tender and succulent all in one mouthful! This is my favourite cut of pork and the end result is wonderful. The cooking temperature may seem high to begin with, but you need that initial blast of heat to get the crackling going – you want it to be good and crispy. If you can, get your butcher to score the belly of pork for you. I love to serve this with baby baked apples or the Roasted Salt & Pepper Pears (see page 116), along with Creamy Mustard Mash (see page 73) and favourite veggies.

Salt & Thyme Crusted Pork Belly

SERVES 4–6

2kg (4lb) thick end belly of pork

2 tablespoons thyme leaves

1 tablespoon sea salt

pepper

Preheat the oven to 240°C/fan 220°C/470°F/Gas Mark 9.

Using a really sharp knife, score the skin of the pork with cuts about 1cm (½ inch) apart. Dry the skin well with kitchen paper.

Grind together the thyme, sea salt and a good grinding of pepper in a mortar with a pestle. Using your hands, rub the mixture firmly over the pork skin, getting right into the cuts.

Roast for 45 minutes, then reduce the oven temperature to 160°C/fan 150°C/325°F/Gas Mark 3 and roast for a further 2½–3 hours until the crackling is a deep golden brown and the meat is almost falling apart.

Remove the crackling before carving the meat into thick slices.

This is a quick pie to make, as it's using lean and tender meat.
The dairy-free puff pastry lid is cooked separately while the
meat is cooking in a rich juniper and wine sauce.

Rich Steak & Venison Pie
with a Black Pepper Crust

SERVES 4

2 tablespoons olive oil

4 red onions, each cut into 8 wedges

275g (9oz) sirloin steak, trimmed and cut into 1-cm (½-inch) strips

275g (9oz) venison fillet, trimmed and cut into 1-cm (½-inch) strips

1 teaspoon sugar

1 teaspoon plain flour

300ml (½ pint) red wine

300ml (½ pint) chicken stock

3 tablespoons balsamic vinegar

8 juniper berries, lightly crushed

1 bay leaf

3 tablespoons port

salt and pepper

PASTRY LID

cracked black pepper, for scattering

375g (12oz) shop-bought ready-rolled dairy-free puff pastry

beaten egg, to glaze

Heat the oil in a frying pan, add the onion wedges and fry gently for 5 minutes. Cover with a lid and cook over a low heat for 15–20 minutes until very soft. Using a slotted spoon, remove from the pan and set to one side.

Add the steak and venison strips to the pan and sear over a high heat for 1–2 minutes on each side. Remove from the pan and set to one side.

Return the onions to the pan and stir in the sugar. Sprinkle in the flour and cook gently for 1 minute. Pour in the red wine, stock and balsamic vinegar, add the juniper berries and bay leaf and bring to the boil. Cook until the liquid has reduced by half and become shiny and slightly sticky.

Meanwhile, preheat the oven to 200°C/fan 180°C/400°F/Gas Mark 6.

Stir the port into the sauce and season to taste with salt and pepper. Add the meat and then divide among 4 small pie dishes, about 10cm (4 inches) in diameter.

Scatter a board with cracked black pepper. Cut out 4 puff pastry lids slightly larger than the pie dish tops and press lightly on both sides on to the pepper. Cut the top of each lid with a sharp knife to form a lattice pattern, taking care not to cut all the way through the pastry. Brush each with beaten egg to glaze and place on a baking sheet.

Cover each pie dish with foil. Bake the pie filling and pastry lids for 15–20 minutes until the lids are risen and browned and the filling piping hot.

Top each pie dish with a peppered pastry lid and serve at once.

This is a deconstructed chilli con carne with a real kick, using black beans and roasted in the oven. Don't buy ready-made burgers, as they are so quick and easy to make. A simple tip is to use wet hands for shaping the burgers.

Hot Black Bean Sweet Chunky Chilli with Steak Burgers & Skinny Chips

SERVES 4

2 red onions, chopped into chunks

1 large red pepper, cored, deseeded and chopped into chunky pieces

2 garlic cloves, unpeeled

4 tablespoons olive oil

400g (13oz) can black beans, rinsed and drained

10 sunblush tomatoes, drained and oil reserved, then chopped

450g (14½oz) tomatoes, chopped into chunky pieces

2 tablespoons caster sugar

2 teaspoons chilli flakes

1 teaspoon sea salt

1 teaspoon cracked black pepper

2 tablespoons balsamic vinegar

2 tablespoons coriander leaves

SKINNY CHIPS

450g (14½oz) potatoes, washed and cut into thin chips

2 tablespoons olive oil

BURGERS

750g (1½lb) lean minced beef

1 tablespoon olive oil

Preheat the oven to 200°C/fan 180°C/400°F/Gas Mark 6.

Place the onions, red pepper and garlic cloves on a large lipped baking sheet, drizzle with half the oil and roast for 10 minutes.

Meanwhile, toss together the black beans and sunblush tomatoes and their oil in a large bowl, season with pepper and set to one side.

Remove the vegetables from the oven. Add the fresh tomatoes and sprinkle over the sugar, chilli flakes, sea salt, cracked black pepper and half the balsamic vinegar. Return to the oven and roast for a further 10–15 minutes or until the tomatoes look lightly charred.

For the skinny chips, spread the chipped potatoes out on a baking sheet lined with baking parchment, drizzle with the oil and toss to coat. Season well with salt and pepper, add to the oven and cook for 20–25 minutes until golden and crisp.

Meanwhile, make the burgers. Place the minced beef in a bowl, season well with salt and pepper and mix thoroughly with your hands. Divide the mixture into 4 and shape into burgers. Set to one side.

Once the roasted vegetables are ready, remove from the oven, mix with the black bean mixture and dress with the remaining oil and balsamic vinegar. Set to one side.

To cook the burgers, heat a griddle pan until really hot. Rub the burgers all over with the olive oil, add to the hot pan and cook for 3–4 minutes until lightly charred. Turn over and cook for a further 3–4 minutes for medium.

To serve, scatter the coriander over the chilli and serve with the burgers and the skinny chips.

The
Clean
Bake

This soft-textured loaf flavoured with meltingly sweet onions is delicious warm from the oven, or toast it for a superb bacon butty.

Caramelized Onion & Spelt Flatbread

MAKES 2 LOAVES

250g (8oz) spelt flour

450g (14½oz) strong white flour, plus extra for dusting

2 teaspoons salt

7g (¼oz) sachet fast-action yeast

400ml (14fl oz) warm water

4 tablespoons olive oil, plus extra for oiling and brushing

2 teaspoons clear honey

sea salt, for sprinkling (optional)

CARAMELIZED ONIONS

2 tablespoons olive oil

2 large onions, finely sliced

Sift the flours into a large bowl and then stir in the salt and yeast. Make a well in the centre of the flour mixture. Mix together the measurement water, oil and honey in a jug, then pour into the well.

Using a flat-bladed knife, draw the flour mixture in from the sides to form a soft dough.

Knead the dough on a lightly floured surface for about 10 minutes until smooth and elastic.

Place the dough in a lightly oiled large bowl, cover with clingfilm and leave to rise in a warm place for about 1 hour or until doubled in size.

Meanwhile, for the caramelized onions, heat the oil in a nonstick frying pan and add the onions. Cover with a lid and cook over a very gentle heat for 15 minutes, stirring occasionally. Remove the lid, turn up the heat and cook the onions for a further 5 minutes or until lightly golden. Remove from the heat and set to one side to cool.

Tip the risen dough out on to a lightly floured surface and knock back with a firm kneading. Flatten the dough out into a large oval and spoon over the cooled onions. Fold the dough over the onions and knead into the dough until evenly distributed.

Divide the dough in half and roll each piece into a large oval about 1cm (½ inch) thick. Place each oval on baking parchment and place on a baking sheet.

Make 2 rows of diagonal slashes in each loaf, then open out the slashes to make large holes in the dough. Brush the dough lightly with olive oil, dust with flour and sprinkle over a little sea salt if you like. Set aside for 10–15 minutes or until the loaves look puffy.

Meanwhile, preheat the oven to 200°C/fan 180°C/400°F/Gas Mark 6.

Bake the breads for 15–20 minutes until golden. Remove from the oven and transfer to a wire rack to cool slightly.

There's something about those little dimples of dough filled with olive oil, sprigs of rosemary and sea salt crystals that just sing summer. This bread really impresses everyone I make it for. It's best eaten warm or on the day that you baked it – don't refrigerate it.

Focaccia with Rosemary

MAKES 2 LOAVES

30g (1oz) fresh yeast

450ml (¾ pint) warm water

680g (1lb 6oz) strong white flour, plus extra for dusting

2 teaspoons salt

4 tablespoons olive oil, plus extra for oiling

TO FINISH

2 tablespoons olive oil

1½ teaspoons coarse sea salt

rosemary sprigs, for scattering

Dissolve the yeast in a little of the measurement water in a jug.

Sift the flour into a large bowl and stir in the salt. Make a well in the centre of the flour and pour in the yeast mixture along with the oil and the remaining measurement water.

Using a flat-bladed knife, draw the flour in from the sides to form a soft dough.

Knead the dough on a lightly floured surface for about 10 minutes until smooth and elastic.

Place the dough in a lightly oiled large bowl, cover with clingfilm and leave to rise in a warm place for about 1½ hours or until doubled in size.

Meanwhile, preheat the oven to 210°C/fan 190°C/425°F/Gas Mark 7.

Tip the risen dough out on to a lightly floured surface and knock back with a firm kneading. Roll it out into 2 long ovals, about 28cm (11 inches) long. Place on a baking sheet, cover with a clean cloth and allow to prove until it looks puffy – this will take approximately 15 minutes, depending on the temperature of the room.

When proved, use your fingertips to form dimples in the dough. To finish, brush the dough with the olive oil, sprinkle with the sea salt and scatter with rosemary sprigs.

Bake for 10–15 minutes, then reduce the heat to 200°C/fan 180°C/400°F/Gas Mark 6 and bake for a further 25–30 minutes until golden and cooked through. Remove from the oven and transfer to a wire rack to cool slightly.

This dairy- and gluten-free Mediterranean batter bread is a storecupboard hero for when friends pop in and you want to impress with an unusual, tasty nibble. Serve torn into strips on a board with some White Bean Creamy Hummus & Dukkah (see page 62). This is also fab served with soups, tagines and curries.

Thyme, Garlic & Chilli Socca

SERVES 4

85g (3¼oz) gram flour

2 tablespoons chopped thyme leaves

2 garlic cloves, crushed

1 chilli, deseeded and finely chopped

225ml (7½fl oz) water

3 tablespoons olive oil

salt and pepper

Place the flour, thyme, garlic, chilli, measurement water, 1 tablespoon of the oil and salt and pepper in a bowl and whisk to a smooth batter. Leave to stand for 30 minutes.

Meanwhile, preheat the oven to 200°C/fan 180°C/400°F/Gas Mark 6.

Heat a heavy roasting tin or shallow baking tray in the oven. When really hot, carefully remove from the oven, add 1 tablespoon of the remaining olive oil and swirl to coat the base. Quickly but carefully pour in the batter and return to the oven for 5 minutes.

While the is batter is baking, preheat your grill to high. After 5 minutes, remove the roasting tin from the oven and drizzle with the remaining olive oil. Place under the grill for 4–5 minutes or until the batter begins to brown.

Remove the bread from under the grill, tear into strips and pile on to a warm plate or a board to serve.

Figs and pepper are the perfect combination. You'll need cracked black pepper for this recipe and not fine black pepper – simply grind it coarsely from the pepper mill and be generous! If you can, eat the bread while it's still warm from the oven.

Cracked Black Pepper & Figgy Bread

SERVES 6

680g (1lb 6oz) strong white flour, plus extra for dusting

2 teaspoons cracked black pepper

2 teaspoons salt

7g (¼oz) sachet fast-action dried yeast

400ml (14fl oz) warm water

2 tablespoons olive oil, plus extra for oiling

350g (11½oz) ready-to-eat dried figs, roughly chopped

Sift the flour into a large bowl and then stir in the pepper, salt and yeast. Make a well in the centre of the flour mixture and pour in the measurement water and oil.

Using a flat-bladed knife, draw the flour mixture in from the sides to form a soft dough.

Knead the dough on a lightly floured surface for about 10 minutes until smooth and elastic.

Place the dough in a lightly oiled large bowl, cover with clingfilm and leave to rise in a warm place for about 1 hour or until doubled in size.

Meanwhile, preheat the oven to 200°C/fan 180°C/400°F/Gas Mark 6. Lightly flour a baking sheet.

Tip the risen dough out on to a lightly floured surface and knock back with a firm kneading. Flatten the dough out into a large oval and scatter over the chopped figs. Fold the dough over the figs and knead into the dough until evenly distributed.

Shape the dough into an oval and place on the prepared baking sheet. Using scissors, roughly slash the top of the loaf.

Bake for 45–50 minutes until golden. Remove from the oven and transfer to a wire rack to cool slightly.

Bread doesn't come simpler or quicker than these two recipes! Both are best served warm, straight from the tin or pan.

Bacon & Sage Cornbread

SERVES 4–6

125g (4oz) bacon lardons

125g (4oz) plain flour

175g (6oz) instant dried polenta

1 tablespoon baking powder

1 tablespoon caster sugar

250ml (8fl oz) almond milk

2 free-range eggs, beaten

4 tablespoons rapeseed oil, plus extra for oiling

2 tablespoons chopped sage

2 teaspoons chilli flakes

Preheat the oven to 200°C/fan 180°C/400°F/Gas Mark 6. Oil a 20-cm (8-inch) square shallow tin and line with baking parchment.

Heat a small frying pan, add the lardons and cook until golden. Drain and set aside.

Mix together the flour, polenta, baking powder and sugar in a bowl and season well with salt and pepper. Add all the remaining ingredients, including the lardons, and stir together.

Pour the mixture into the prepared tin and bake for 20 minutes.

Rest the cornbread in the tin for 5 minutes before turning out. Cut into chunks and serve warm.

Cheese & Chive Soda Bread

MAKES 12 RUSTIC ROLLS

450g (14½oz) plain flour

2 tablespoons baking powder

4 tablespoons chopped chives

4 tablespoons mixed seeds, such as pumpkin and sunflower

125g (4oz) dairy-free Cheddar-style cheese, finely grated

4 tablespoons olive oil

300ml (½ pint) almond milk (see page 177), plus extra if needed

Preheat the oven to 210°C/fan 190°C/425°F/Gas Mark 7. Line a baking sheet with baking parchment.

Sift the flour and baking powder into a large bowl and season well with salt and pepper. Add the chives, seeds and cheese and mix well.

Combine the oil and milk in a jug, then gently mix in to the flour mixture to form a soft dough, adding extra milk if necessary.

Divide the dough into 12 even-sized pieces and roll each into a ball on a lightly floured surface. Arrange the dough balls on the lined baking sheet. Bake for 25 minutes until puffed and golden. Serve warm.

*These breadsticks are perfect for dipping into creamy hummus
(see page 160 for homemade). I also like to wrap them with
air-cured ham to serve as a posh nibble.*

Poppy Seed Grissini

MAKES ABOUT 32

500g (1lb) strong white flour, plus extra for dusting

7g (¼oz) sachet fast-action dried yeast

1 teaspoon salt

300ml (½ pint) warm water

3 tablespoons olive oil

beaten egg, to glaze

3 tablespoons poppy seeds

Sift the flour into a large bowl and then stir in the yeast and salt. Make a well in the centre of the flour mixture and pour in the measurement water and oil.

Using a flat-bladed knife, draw the flour mixture in from the sides to form a firm but slightly sticky dough.

Knead the dough on a lightly floured surface for about 10 minutes until smooth and elastic.

Place the dough in a large clean bowl, cover with clingfilm and leave to rest for 30 minutes.

Tip the dough out on to a lightly floured surface and knead for a further 10 minutes.

Meanwhile, preheat the oven to 200°C/fan 180°C/400°F/Gas Mark 6, and lightly flour 2 large baking sheets.

Roll and shape the dough into a rectangle about 20cm x 30cm (8 inches x 12 inches) or A4 size and 1cm (½ inch) thick. Cut the rectangle into 4 quarters, then cut each quarter into 8 equal strips. Stretch each strip to about 20cm (8 inches) in length.

Place the strips on the prepared baking sheets about 1.5cm (¾ inch) apart, brush with beaten egg to glaze and scatter over the poppy seeds.

Bake the breadsticks for 15–18 minutes until golden and firm. Remove from the oven and transfer to a wire rack to cool.

I first tried this at a dairy-intolerant friend's birthday party. I couldn't believe how light, moist and deliciously rich a sponge could be. It's so easy to make and you can change the flavour of the sponge by adding lemon or orange rind, coffee or almond extract. However, my favourite version has to be this classic vanilla bean-flavoured one, filled with strawberry jam.

Vanilla Bean & Olive Oil Sandwich Cake

SERVES 8

5 free-range eggs

150g (5oz) caster sugar

pinch of salt

2 teaspoons vanilla bean paste

175ml (6fl oz) olive oil

125g (4oz) self-raising flour

½ teaspoon baking powder

4 tablespoons strawberry jam

vanilla caster sugar, for sprinkling

TO SERVE

raspberries or strawberries

dairy-free cream

Preheat the oven to 190°C/fan 170°C/375°F/Gas Mark 5. Line the base of 2 x 20-cm (8-inch) sandwich tins with baking parchment.

Place the eggs and sugar in a large bowl and, using a hand-held electric whisk, beat until thick and mousse-like. Add the salt and vanilla bean paste.

Whisk in the oil in a steady stream, then sift in the flour and baking powder and quickly fold in.

Spoon the mixture into the prepared tins and bake for 25 minutes until pale golden and just firm.

Allow to cool in the tins for 5 minutes. They will fall slightly while cooling, but don't panic – this is normal. Remove from the tins and leave to cool on a wire rack.

Sandwich the cakes together with the jam and place on a serving plate. Sprinkle the top with vanilla caster sugar and serve with a pile of fresh, sweet raspberries or strawberries and a jug of dairy-free cream.

Oh my goodness, these moreish muffin-type cakes are wonderfully light and so, so moist! These are fabulous simply served straight from the oven, or allow them to cool and top with dairy-free cream cheese frosting as below.

Carrot & Walnut Muffelettas

MAKES 16

225g (7½oz) self-raising flour

2 teaspoons baking powder

225g (7½oz) dairy-free spread

4 free-range eggs

225g (7½oz) caster sugar

grated rind of 1 large orange

140g (4½oz) peeled and coarsely grated carrot (about 1 large carrot)

100g (3½oz) walnuts, roughly chopped

FROSTING

225g (7½oz) dairy-free cream cheese

1 tablespoon icing sugar, sifted, or to taste

ground cinnamon, for sprinkling

Preheat the oven to 190°C/fan 170°C/375°F/Gas Mark 5. Line 8 holes of a muffin tin with paper cases.

Place all the ingredients except the walnuts in a food processor and whizz until well mixed.

Add the walnuts and pulse until well combined.

Fill the muffin cases about half full with the mixture and bake for 18 minutes or until golden and just firm.

Meanwhile, to make the frosting, mix together the cream cheese and icing sugar in a bowl.

Remove the muffelettas from the oven and allow to cool a little. Top each with the frosting and sprinkle each with a little ground cinnamon.

These are grown-up cupcakes – dark chocolate with a hit of lime, topped with a glossy fondant chilli chocolate sauce. They take no time at all to bake, but don't forget them, as you want them to be a little bit squidgy in the centre.

Lime Chocolate Cupcakes with Chilli Fondant Sauce

MAKES 8

150g (5oz) dairy-free spread, plus extra for greasing

150g (5oz) caster sugar

grated rind of 1 unwaxed lime

2 large free-range eggs, beaten

125g (4oz) self-raising flour

50g (2oz) dairy-free cocoa powder

3 tablespoons hazelnut milk

CHILLI FONDANT SAUCE

3 tablespoons golden syrup

100g (3½oz) dairy-free plain dark chocolate, broken into pieces

1–2 teaspoons Tabasco sauce, to taste

1 tablespoon finely chopped pistachio nuts (optional)

Preheat the oven to 200°C/fan 180°C/400°F/Gas Mark 6. Grease 8 holes of a large, nonstick muffin tin.

Place the spread, sugar and lime rind in a food processor and whizz together until pale and creamy. With the food processor running, gradually add the eggs. Sift together the flour and cocoa. Add to the processor with the hazelnut milk and pulse briefly until just mixed in.

Spoon the mixture into the prepared muffin holes and bake for about 10–12 minutes until just firm but still squidgy in the centre.

Meanwhile, for the sauce, place the golden syrup and chocolate in a small saucepan over a low heat and stir until melted and smooth. Add the Tabasco sauce to taste. Set aside to cool.

Remove the cupcakes from the oven and allow to cool in the tins for 5 minutes, then transfer to a wire rack.

Place the cupcakes on a serving plate and top each with the cooled fondant. Sprinkle over the pistachios, if using, and serve.

These Cinnamon & Orange Cookies are the perfect spiced bites to enjoy with your coffee. The Cocoa Crumble Cookies (see below) are rich in cocoa, not too sweet, and best served on the day of baking.

Cinnamon & Orange Cookies

MAKES 20

125g (4oz) dairy-free spread

50g (2oz) soft light brown sugar

150g (5oz) self-raising flour, plus extra for dusting

3 teaspoons ground cinnamon

grated rind of 1 orange

sifted icing sugar, for dusting

Preheat the oven to 190°C/fan 170°C/375°F/Gas Mark 5. Lightly flour 2 baking sheets.

Beat together the spread and sugar in a bowl until light and fluffy. Sift in the flour and cinnamon, add the orange rind and mix well.

Divide the mixture into 20, roll with your hands into balls and place on the prepared baking sheets. Flatten the cookies with a wet fork.

Bake for 15 minutes. Remove from the oven and allow to cool slightly on the sheets before transferring to a wire rack. Dust with icing sugar and serve warm or cold.

Cocoa Crumble Cookies

MAKES 10

125g (4oz) dairy-free spread

65g (2½oz) caster sugar

125g (4oz) self-raising flour, plus extra for dusting

30g (1oz) dairy-free cocoa powder, plus extra for dusting

85g (3¼oz) dairy-free plain dark chocolate, roughly chopped

Beat together the spread and sugar in a bowl until light and fluffy. Sift in the flour and cocoa and mix well, then stir in the chopped chocolate. Roll the mixture into a thick cylinder, wrap in clingfilm and chill in the refrigerator for 1 hour.

Meanwhile, preheat the oven to 190°C/fan 170°C/375°F/Gas Mark 5. Line 2 baking sheets with baking parchment.

Cut the mixture into 10 slices and place on the prepared baking sheets. Flatten the cookies with the back of a floured fork.

Bake for 18–20 minutes. Remove from the oven and allow to cool on the sheets for 10 minutes before transferring to a wire rack. Dust with cocoa to serve.

*This deliciously moist coconut cake is also wheat free. Serve as a
teatime cake, or for a sophisticated pudding, serve with a fruit salad,
as here, or just raspberries or mango, or with a lemon sorbet.*

Coconut & Lime Cake

SERVES 8–10

225g (7½oz) desiccated coconut

225g (7½oz) dairy-free spread,
softened, plus extra for greasing

225g (7½oz) caster sugar

grated rind and juice of 2 unwaxed
limes

3 free-range eggs, beaten

125g (4oz) rice flour

1½ teaspoons gluten-free baking
powder

4 tablespoons icing sugar

FRUIT SALAD

4 passion fruit, halved and seeds
and juice scooped out

1 large mango, stoned, peeled and
cut into chunks

grated rind of 1 unwaxed lime

Preheat the oven to 160°C/fan 150°C/325°F/Gas Mark 3. Lightly grease
and flour a 23-cm (9-inch) round springform cake tin.

Place the coconut in a food processor and process for about 2 minutes
until fine in texture. Remove and set to one side.

Add the spread, caster sugar and lime rind to the food processor
and blitz until pale and creamy. Gradually add the eggs, pulsing
the machine constantly. Pulse in the coconut, rice flour and baking
powder until well mixed.

Spoon into the prepared tin and level the top with the back of a
spoon. Bake for about 45 minutes or until lightly golden and just firm.

Meanwhile, place the lime juice in a small bowl, sift in the icing sugar
and mix well.

Remove the cake from oven and allow to cool for 10 minutes. Spoon
over the lime mixture and leave to cool in the tin for 20 minutes.

Remove the cake from the tin and place on a serving plate.

For the fruit salad, combine the passion fruit, mango and lime rind
in a serving bowl and serve with the cake.

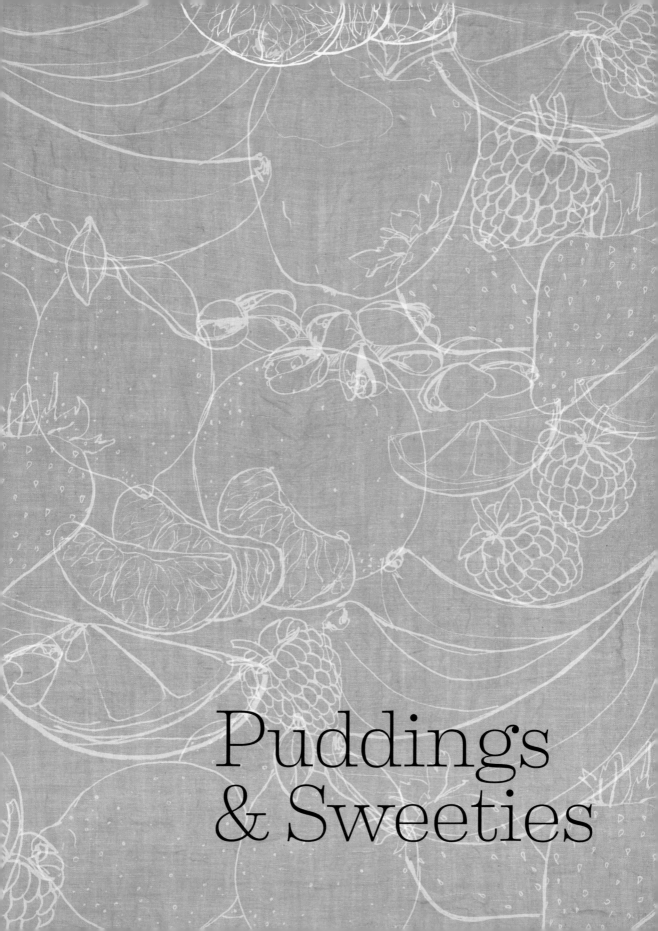

Puddings
& Sweeties

A bubbling hot, upside-down banana toffee extravaganza! A touch of sea salt in this sweet, sticky pudding really works. Classic tarte tatin is made with caramelized apples and a sweet shortcrust pastry, but for this cheats' version, ready-made dairy-free puff pastry works best.

Salted Caramel Banana Toffee Tatin

SERVES 6

3 tablespoons rapeseed oil

85g (3¼oz) light muscovado sugar

good pinch of sea salt

7 medium bananas, cut into 2.5-cm (1-inch) thick slices

375g (12oz) shop-bought dairy-free puff pastry

plain flour, for dusting

2 limes, cut into wedges

Preheat the oven to 200°C/fan 180°C/400°F/Gas Mark 6.

Heat the oil and sugar in a 25-cm (10-inch) nonstick, ovenproof frying pan and simmer for 2 minutes until well dissolved and bubbling hot – it will slightly separate, but do not panic. Sprinkle in the salt.

Carefully place the banana slices in the pan on top of the caramel in a single layer, making sure they are tightly pushed together.

Roll out the pastry on a lightly floured surface to form a square. Using a sharp knife, cut out a round slightly larger than the pan. Lift the pastry over the bananas like a blanket, allowing the edges to fall into the side.

Place the pan on a baking sheet and bake for about 35 minutes until bubbling hot and the puff pastry is golden and cooked.

To serve, remove from the oven and allow to stand for 4–5 minutes before carefully turning out on to a large serving plate with the bananas facing up. Serve with the lime wedges for squeezing over.

Rice pudding is one of my favourite comfort puddings of all time. This is made all the more special by the addition of coconut cream and zesty lime. Serve with griddled pineapple or a dollop of homemade Rhubarb & Vanilla Jam or the Summer Pudding Jam (see opposite).

Coconut Rice Pudding with Griddled Pineapple

SERVES 4

225g (7½oz) pudding rice, washed

500ml (17fl oz) water

300ml (½ pint) coconut cream

125g (4oz) caster sugar

grated rind of 1 unwaxed lime

1 small pineapple, skin removed, cored and cut into small wedges

1 tablespoon small mint leaves

Place the rice and measurement water in a saucepan over a medium heat and bring to the boil. Cover with a lid and reduce the heat to low. Cook for 10–12 minutes or until the water has been absorbed and the rice is almost cooked – add a little extra water if needed.

Stir in the coconut cream, sugar and lime rind, re-cover the pan and continue cooking over a low heat, stirring occasionally, for 10–12 minutes until thick, creamy and cooked.

Meanwhile, heat a griddle pan over a high heat, add the pineapple wedges and cook for a few minutes on each side or until caramelized.

To serve, spoon the rice into warmed serving bowls, top each with the hot griddled pineapple and scatter over a few small mint leaves.

This Summer Pudding Jam goes well with the Meringue Nougats (see page 159), while the Rhubarb & Vanilla Jam (see below) is perfect with scones or stirred into porridge for a breakfast treat.

Summer Pudding Jam

SERVES 6

juice of 1 orange

85g (3½oz) caster sugar

175g (6oz) raspberries

125g (4oz) blackberries, blackcurrants or redcurrants

350g (11½oz) strawberries, hulled and halved if large

Place the orange juice and sugar in a shallow pan. Heat over a medium heat until the sugar has dissolved, then bring to the boil and reduce by half.

Add 125g (4oz) of the raspberries and crush with a masher. Cook until syrupy, jammy and sticky.

Add the blackberries or currants and toss in the hot sauce for 2 minutes, then add the strawberries and remaining raspberries and toss in the hot sauce.

Pour out on to a large tray and allow to cool, then spoon into a sterilized jar. Keep in the refrigerator and eat within 3–4 days.

Rhubarb & Vanilla Jam

MAKES ONE 1-LITRE (1¾-PINT) JAR

1kg (2lb) rhubarb, trimmed and cut into 3-cm (1¼-inch) lengths

1kg (2lb) jam sugar

juice of 1 lemon

grated rind of 1 orange

1 vanilla pod, split

Place the rhubarb and sugar in a preserving pan or wok and heat over a low heat until all the sugar has dissolved.

Add the remaining ingredients and stir well. Turn up the heat and bring to the boil. Use a spoon to skim the surface, then allow the jam to boil rapidly for 10–15 minutes. To test the consistency of jam, place a couple of saucers in the freezer. Spoon a little of the jam on to a chilled saucer and allow to cool slightly, then run your finger through it – it should wrinkle slightly.

Carefully pour into a sterilized 1-litre (1¾-pint) Kilner or other preserving jar, removing the vanilla pod, and seal straight away, then set to one side to cool. Keep in a cool, dark place for up to 3 months. Once opened, keep in the refrigerator.

Full of flavour, juicy and sweet, these nectarines are my modern take on peach melba. They can be served with the Meringue Nougats (see below), or with dairy-free ice-cream.

Roasted Vanilla Nectarines with Sweet Wine & Berry Sauce

SERVES 4–6

125g (4oz) caster sugar

½ vanilla pod, split and seeds scraped out

6 ripe nectarines, halved and stoned

grated rind and juice of 1 large orange

7 tablespoons sweet dessert wine

125g (4oz) blackberries

125g (4oz) raspberries, mixed with 1 tablespoon water

Preheat the oven to 200°C/fan 180°C/400°F/Gas Mark 6.

Toss together the sugar and the vanilla seeds and pod in a bowl.

Place the nectarines in a roasting tray and scatter over the vanilla sugar. Pour over the orange rind and juice and 5 tablespoons of the wine. Roast the nectarines for 30 minutes until just soft.

Turn the nectarines into a colander over a bowl to collect any juices. Allow to cool for a few minutes before transferring to a serving dish.

Add the juices from the nectarines and remaining wine to a shallow pan, bring to the boil and reduce to 4 tablespoons. Add the berries and cook for 30 seconds, then spoon the berry sauce over the nectarines.

Meringue Nougats

SERVES 4

4 egg whites

225g (7½oz) caster sugar

2 teaspoons cornflour

2 teaspoons white wine vinegar

200g (7oz) flaked almonds, toasted

1 vanilla pod, split and seeds scraped out

Preheat the oven to 140°C/fan 130°C/285°F/Gas Mark 1. Line 2 baking sheets with baking parchment.

Whisk the egg whites in a large bowl until stiff. Whisk in the sugar, 1 tablespoon at a time, until it is all incorporated and the mixture is stiff enough to stand a spoon up in. Fold in the cornflour, vinegar, almonds and the scraped out vanilla seeds.

Using 2 tablespoons, roughly mould 12 oval-shaped meringues on to the baking sheets. Bake for about 35 minutes. When cooked, remove from the oven and allow to cool. Keep in an airtight tin until needed.

This mousse is very rich and creamy and you won't be disappointed. The secret ingredient, although you'd never guess, are prunes – dried plums. Serve it with chopped pistachios and plenty of grated chocolate.

Plummy Chocolate Mousse with Pistachios

SERVES 4–6

175g (6oz) ready-to-eat vanilla prunes

200ml (7fl oz) water

2 tablespoons brandy (optional)

125g (4oz) dairy-free plain dark chocolate, broken into pieces, plus extra for grating

3 egg whites

4 teaspoons caster sugar

2 tablespoons pistachio nuts, roughly chopped

Place the prunes in a saucepan and add the measurement water to barely cover them. Simmer gently for about 15 minutes until very, very soft.

Transfer to a small food processor with any remaining cooking liquid and the brandy, if using, and blend to a smooth purée.

Place the chocolate in a small heatproof bowl over a saucepan of gently simmering water and stir with a spatula until the chocolate has melted. Remove from heat and allow to cool for 5 minutes.

Beat the egg whites in a large bowl until just stiff, then add the sugar and beat again until thick and glossy.

Stir the melted chocolate into the prune purée and beat together well.

Using a large metal spoon, quickly stir a spoonful of the beaten egg white into the chocolate mixture – this will help to loosen the mixture. Add the remaining egg whites to the mixture and fold in.

Spoon the mousse into 4 or 6 medium-sized espresso cups and chill for at least 1 hour. Sprinkle over the pistachios and some grated chocolate just before serving.

Scrumptious and moist, this cake is also very versatile, as you can change the fruits as the seasons go by – this version with rhubarb is good for spring, while plump gooseberries are lovely in summer, halved and stoned plums in autumn and peeled, cored and sliced pears in winter. Delicious served warm with Homemade Custard Sauce flavoured with cardamom (see page 169). Any leftovers can be served with afternoon tea.

Rhubarb, Almond & Orange Pudding Cake

SERVES 6

rapeseed oil, for oiling

225g (7½oz) dairy-free spread

225g (7½oz) caster sugar, plus extra for sprinkling

3 free-range eggs, beaten

200g (7oz) ground almonds

115g (4oz) instant dried polenta

1 teaspoon baking powder

grated rind of 2 oranges

275g (9oz) rhubarb, trimmed and cut into 7-cm (3-inch) thin sticks

Preheat the oven to 190°C/fan 170°C/375°F/Gas Mark 5. Lightly oil a 23-cm (9-inch) round, nonstick springform or sponge cake tin and line the base and side with baking parchment.

Place the spread and sugar in a food processor and whizz together until pale and creamy. With the food processor running, gradually add the eggs.

Mix together the ground almonds, polenta, baking powder and orange rind, add to the processor and pulse briefly to combine.

Spoon the mixture into the prepared cake tin and lay the rhubarb sticks on the surface like the spokes of a wheel. Sprinkle with a little extra caster sugar and bake for about 1 hour until firm and golden.

Allow the cake to stand for 20 minutes before serving.

What could be more heavenly than an oozy, saucy chocolate pudding? This is good enough to serve for any occasion – straight from the oven with the orange-flavoured coconut cream, as the longer you leave it sitting, the less saucy it becomes.

Mega Saucy Chocolate Pud with Orange Coconut Cream

SERVES 6–8

100g (3½oz) dairy-free spread, plus extra for greasing

200g (7oz) caster sugar

2 free-range eggs, beaten

150ml (¼ pint) dairy-free milk

200g (7oz) self-raising flour

25g (1oz) dairy-free cocoa powder

TOPPING

175g (6oz) light muscovado sugar

85g (3¼oz) dairy-free cocoa powder, sifted

600ml (1 pint) very hot water

COCONUT CREAM

400ml (14oz) can full-fat coconut milk, chilled in the refrigerator overnight or for 24 hours

grated rind of 1 orange

Preheat the oven to 190°C/fan 170°C/375°F/Gas Mark 5. Lightly grease a shallow, ovenproof dish about 2 litres (3½ pints) in capacity.

Beat together the spread and caster sugar in a bowl until light and fluffy. Add the eggs and milk and beat well. Sift in the flour and cocoa powder and fold in until combined. Spread the mixture into the prepared dish.

For the topping, mix together the muscovado sugar and cocoa powder and sprinkle over the pudding mixture. Gently pour over the measurement water to cover and bake for about 35–40 minutes or until the pudding has risen and is just set but still really saucy.

Meanwhile, open the chilled can of coconut milk. Scoop the coconut cream that has solidified at the top of the can into a bowl, leaving behind the watery liquid at the bottom. Add the orange rind to the bowl and whisk briefly until lightly whipped.

Serve the hot pudding straight away with the coconut cream.

Ice cream in a whizz! Serve in cornets or in coupes with a wafer, or fab with the Roasted Vanilla Nectarines with Sweet Wine & Berry Sauce (see page 168). Ready-frozen fruits can be used instead of frozen fresh ones, but the end result will never be as good.

Raspberry & Banana
Instant Ice Cream

SERVES 4

2 ripe bananas
225g (7½oz) fresh raspberries, frozen
3 tablespoons dairy-free single cream
3 tablespoons icing sugar

Peel and roughly chop the bananas, then place in the freezer for 1 hour or until semi-frozen.

Add the frozen banana with the raspberries to a food processor and blitz until just smooth.

Add the cream and sugar and pulse until combined.

Serve straight away, or scrape into a freezer-proof container and freeze until needed.

An apple pie with attitude, the rosemary and cider really make this trad pie something else. As the polenta pastry crust cooks, it moulds itself over the apple halves. The final sprinkling of caster sugar is essential as it creates a lovely crust. Serve with Homemade Custard Sauce or Vanilla Ice Cream (see opposite).

Cider Baked Apple Pie with Polenta Pastry

SERVES 6

140g (4½oz) plain flour, plus extra for dusting

50g (2oz) instant dried polenta

pinch of salt

100g (3½oz) dairy-free spread

1 large egg, beaten

about 1–2 tablespoons cold water

caster sugar, for sprinkling

FILLING

6 large dessert apples, peeled, cored and halved

150ml (¼ pint) fruity cider

50g (2oz) light soft brown sugar

1 rosemary sprig

Preheat the oven to 200°C/fan 180°C/400°F/Gas Mark 6.

Sift the flour into a bowl and stir in the polenta and salt. Add the spread in small pieces and lightly rub in with your fingertips until the mixture resembles fine breadcrumbs. Alternatively, place the ingredients in a food processor and whizz together. Gently mix in the egg and enough of the measurement water to bind the pastry dough together. Wrap in clingfilm and chill in the refrigerator for 30 minutes.

Place the apples cut side down in a shallow, round dish about 23cm (9 inches) in diameter. Pour the cider over the apples, then sprinkle with the brown sugar and tuck in the rosemary sprig.

Roll out the pastry on a lightly floured surface until it is large enough to lay over the apples as a blanket. Carefully lift the pastry over the apples, roughly trim the edge and tuck inside the dish. Lightly sprinkle the pastry with the caster sugar.

Bake the pie for 40–45 minutes until the apples are softened and cooked and the pastry crust is golden and crisp.

Nothing beats homemade custard. The flavouring for this recipe is traditional vanilla but various other infusions can be used instead, such as grated orange rind, rosemary sprigs or a handful of crushed cardamom seeds.

Homemade Custard Sauce

SERVES 4

450ml (¾ pint) almond milk (see page 177 for homemade)

1 vanilla pod, split

4 egg yolks

40g (1½oz) caster sugar

2 teaspoons cornflour

4 tablespoons dairy-free single cream

Heat the almond milk with the vanilla pod in a pan and very gently bring to the boil. Remove from the heat and allow to infuse for 10 minutes.

Beat together the egg yolks, sugar and cornflour in a bowl.

Gradually pour the infused milk on to the egg yolk mixture, stirring constantly. Strain the mixture through a sieve, removing the vanilla pod, back into the cleaned pan.

Return the pan to a very low heat and stir constantly until the mixture thickens enough to coat the back of a spoon, but do not allow to boil.

Strain through a sieve into a clean bowl and stir in the cream.

Vanilla Ice Cream
To turn this recipe into a simple ice cream, allow the custard to cool and add 2 tablespoons sifted icing sugar before pouring into an ice cream maker and churning according to the manufacturer's instructions. Alternatively, turn into a shallow freezer-proof dish, cover and freeze for about 4–6 hours until just frozen. Remove from the freezer and blitz in a food processor until smooth. Return to the freezer until needed.

Frangipane is a term used for a rich almond paste, but in this recipe ground walnuts are used instead of almonds: simply place walnut pieces in a food processor and blitz until fine. The walnut paste makes a perfect base for the plums to stick to and keeps everything moist. Adding rice flour gives the pastry a lovely shortbread texture.

Frangipane Plum Tart

SERVES A GENEROUS 6!

750g (1½lb) plums, halved, stoned and each half cut into 4

sifted icing sugar, for dusting

PASTRY

250g (8oz) plain flour, plus extra for dusting

85g (3¼oz) rice flour

200g (7oz) dairy-free spread

50g (2oz) caster sugar

grated rind of 1 orange

1 large egg, beaten

1–2 tablespoons cold water

FRANGIPANE

100g (3½oz) dairy-free spread

100g (3½oz) caster sugar

1 egg and 1 egg yolk, beaten together

2 tablespoons plain flour

100g (3½oz) ground walnuts

Preheat the oven to 200°C/fan 180°C/400°F/Gas Mark 6. Line a large baking sheet with baking parchment and dust with a little flour.

To make the pastry, sift the flours into a bowl. Add the spread in small pieces and lightly rub in with your fingertips until the mixture resembles fine breadcrumbs. Alternatively, place the ingredients in a food processor and whizz together. Stir in the sugar and orange rind. Gently mix in the egg and enough of the measurement water to bind the pastry dough together. Wrap in clingfilm and chill in the refrigerator for 30 minutes.

Roll out the pastry on a lightly floured surface to a small rectangle. Continue to roll very thinly into a rectangle about 24cm x 36cm (9½ x 14 inches). Transfer to the prepared baking sheet.

For the frangipane, beat together the spread and sugar in a bowl until light and fluffy. Add the eggs a little at a time, beating well between each addition. Fold in the flour and walnuts.

Using a flat-bladed knife, carefully spread the frangipane in a thin, even layer to cover the pastry base, leaving a 1-cm (½-inch) border around the edges.

Arrange the plums evenly in 5 rows and lightly push them into the frangipane.

Bake for 30–35 minutes or until the frangipane is just firm, the pastry golden and the plums bubbling hot.

To serve, dust with icing sugar and slide the tart on the paper on to a large serving board.

Serve these little pots of soft Lemon Posset with Cocoa Crumble Cookies or Cinnamon & Orange Cookies (see page 148). The Sparkling Jellies (below) are simply delicious. You can use any sparkling wine, but for special occasions I like to use Champagne.

Lemon Posset with Strawberries

SERVES 4

400ml (14fl oz) can coconut milk

3 tablespoons caster sugar

grated rind from 1 unwaxed lemon and juice from ½

4 teaspoons cornflour

2 tablespoons cold water

200g (7oz) strawberries, hulled and sliced

sifted icing sugar, for dusting

Pour the coconut milk into a small saucepan and add the sugar and lemon rind. Place over a medium heat and simmer until the sugar has dissolved.

Dissolve the cornflour in the measurement water in a small bowl. Stir the cornflour mixture into the coconut milk and simmer, stirring, for 1 minute. Stir in the lemon juice and allow to cool slightly.

Pour the posset into 4 small jam jars, Kilner or other preserving jars or tumblers. Chill in the refrigerator for 2 hours or until just set. To serve, top each with the strawberries and dust well with icing sugar.

Sparkling Jellies

MAKES 4

3 sheets of leaf gelatine

2 tablespoons caster sugar

450ml (¾ pint) sparkling wine

125g (4oz) blueberries

125g (4oz) raspberries

50g (2oz) small seedless red grapes

Soak the gelatine sheets in a bowl of cold water for 5 minutes.

Meanwhile, place the sugar and 100ml of the sparkling wine in a saucepan and stir over a very low heat until the sugar has dissolved. Pour into a large jug.

Squeeze the gelatine leaves to remove the excess water, then stir them into the warm liquid. Stir in the remaining sparkling wine.

Divide the berries and grapes among 4 glasses. Pour in the wine mixture to just cover. Place the glasses in the refrigerator and leave for about 2 hours or until just set. Serve straight away – the longer the jelly is out of the refrigerator, the more it will soften.

Serve this flourless, rich cake with espresso syrup and a scattering of raspberries for a sophisticated chocolate dessert. Strong coffee and chocolate just go hand in hand – it's one of the best flavour combinations I know – and the addition of polenta gives the cake a unique texture. This cake will keep for at least a week if stored in the refrigerator.

Chocolate Polenta Cake with Espresso Syrup

SERVES 8

rapeseed oil, for oiling

200g (7oz) dairy-free plain dark chocolate, broken into pieces

225g (7½oz) dairy-free spread

225g (7½oz) caster sugar

3 free-range eggs, beaten

200g (7oz) ground almonds

75g (3oz) instant dried polenta

1 teaspoon baking powder

40g (1½oz) dairy-free cocoa powder, sifted

TO FINISH

450ml (¾ pint) strong cafetière coffee or instant espresso

175g (6oz) caster sugar

sifted icing sugar, for dusting

raspberries, to serve

Preheat the oven to 180°C/fan 160°C/350°F/Gas Mark 4. Lightly oil a 28-cm (11-inch) round, nonstick springform cake tin and line the base with baking parchment.

Place the chocolate in a heatproof bowl over a saucepan of gently simmering water and stir with a spatula until the chocolate has melted. Remove from heat and allow to cool for 5 minutes.

Beat together the spread and sugar in a bowl until light and fluffy. Add the eggs a little at a time, beating well between each addition. Fold in the almonds, polenta, baking powder and cocoa, then gently stir in the melted chocolate.

Spoon the mixture into the prepared tin and bake for about 30–35 minutes or until just firm.

Remove the cake from the oven and prick the surface with a thin skewer. Spoon 150ml (¼ pint) of the coffee over the surface of the cake and allow to cool for 45 minutes before removing from the tin.

Place the remaining coffee in a small saucepan, add the caster sugar and simmer for about 5 minutes until syrupy. Allow to cool slightly.

Remove the lining paper from the cake and place the cake on a serving plate. Dust with icing sugar. To plate up restaurant style, using a large hot knife (dipped in boiling water), cut the cake into neat wedges, place on medium-sized plates and sit a small pile of raspberries to the side, then drizzle over a little of the coffee syrup. Or to serve family style, take the cake to the table with a bowl of raspberries and a jug of the warm coffee syrup.

This is a delicious, squidgier version of that family favourite tiffin cake. It's great served as a teatime treat, or cut into smaller pieces and serve with after-dinner coffee. You can replace the apricots with raisins, figs, dates, cherries or whichever is your favourite. For an adult version, add a slug of brandy.

Chocolate & Apricot Fudgy Refrigerator Cake

MAKES 16 SQUARES

150g (5oz) dairy-free spread

5 tablespoons golden syrup

2 tablespoons dairy-free cocoa powder, sifted

200g (7oz) dried apricots, finely chopped

2 nuggets of stem ginger, finely chopped

85g (3¼oz) dairy-free plain dark chocolate, broken into chunks

200g (7oz) dairy-free digestive biscuits

Line a 20-cm (8-inch) square tin with baking parchment.

Place the spread, golden syrup and cocoa powder in a deep saucepan over a medium heat and mix well. Gently bring to the boil and allow to bubble gently for 2 minutes.

Stir in the apricots and ginger, return to the boil and mix well.

Take the pan off the heat and stir in the chocolate.

Place half the digestives in a plastic bag and beat with a rolling pin until fine crumbs, then stir into the mixture.

Place the remaining biscuits in a plastic bag and bash until gently broken into chunks, then stir into the mixture.

Spoon the mixture into the prepared tin and level out. Set aside to cool for 30 minutes.

Run a fork over the top to make it rougher on top. Place in the refrigerator for 4 hours (or overnight, if possible) to set before cutting into squares.

Basics

Almond milk is now available in most supermarkets and health food shops, but making your own is pretty simple – you just need to soak the almonds for at least 1–2 days. The longer you soak the nuts, the creamier and more flavoursome your milk will become.

DIY Fresh Almond Milk

MAKES 500ML (17FL OZ)

150g (5oz) raw almonds

500ml (17fl oz) water

maple syrup, vanilla extract or clear honey, to taste (optional)

Place the almonds in a bowl and cover with cold water. Leave to soak for 1–2 days.

Drain the almonds and rinse well.

Place the almonds and the measurement water in a blender and pulse to break the almonds up. Blend vigorously for 2–3 minutes or until smooth and creamy.

Line a sieve with a piece of muslin. Strain the almond milk through the lined sieve into a jug and squeeze out any excess.

Cover the jug with clingfilm and place in the refrigerator. It will last for up to 2 days and can be sweetened to taste with maple syrup, vanilla extract or honey.

This homemade Cashew Honey Cream is thick and tasty – try it with the Salted Caramel Banana Toffee Tatin (see page 154), on scones or with fresh fruit. Instead of honey, you can add a hit of vanilla bean paste or drizzle of maple syrup for flavour. Crunchy or creamy, the Instant Peanut Butter (below) is delicious. If you fancy a bit of heat, add a pinch or two of chilli flakes to the peanuts.

Cashew Honey Cream

SERVES 4

100g (3½oz) raw cashew nuts

1 tablespoon clear honey

Place the nuts in a small bowl and just cover with cold water. Leave to soak for 2 hours.

Drain the cashews, reserving the soaking liquid. Place the drained cashews in a small food processor along with 6 tablespoons of the reserved liquid and the honey. Whizz for 2–3 minutes until smooth and creamy, adding extra soaking liquid if needed.

Spoon into a serving bowl, cover with clingfilm and chill in the refrigerator until required.

Instant Peanut Butter

SERVES 6

400g (13oz) salted roasted peanuts

1 tablespoon clear honey

4 tablespoons olive or rapeseed oil

Place the peanuts and honey in a food processor and whizz together for 1 minute.

With the food processor running, add the oil in a steady stream, then whizz for a further 3–4 minutes depending on how crunchy or smooth you want it.

Scrape into a sterilized Kilner or other preserving jar or a jam jar, seal and store in the refrigerator until needed. Will keep in the refrigerator for 2 weeks.

Spread this thickly on to Meringue Nougats (see page 159) for sandwiching together – what could be more heavenly! I like to add the brandy, as it makes it truly special. Other options are to spread it on thick toast or simply heat gently and use as a fondue dipping sauce for strawberries and cherries or as a rich chocolate sauce – the hazelnuts can always be omitted. If you want a hint of spice, a pinch of chilli flakes in with the sugar works well.

Hazelnut Chocolate Spread

MAKES ONE 400ML (14OZ) JAR

250ml (8fl oz) dairy-free single cream

125g (4oz) plain dark chocolate, broken into pieces

25g (1oz) caster sugar

100g (3½oz) whole hazelnuts, toasted and skins rubbed off with a tea towel

1 tablespoon brandy (optional)

Place the cream, chocolate and sugar in a saucepan over a gentle heat and bring to the boil, stirring constantly. Stir in the hazelnuts and brandy, if using.

Pour into a sterilized Kilner or other preserving jar or a jam jar and allow to cool before sealing. It will keep up to 1 week in the refrigerator.

Juniper is the perfect match for red cabbage and cranberries. Serve this robust chutney with game such as pheasant or venison, or even with simple bangers and mash.

Cranberry, Red Cabbage & Juniper Jam

SERVES 4–6

2 tablespoons olive oil

2 large red onions, finely sliced

225g (7½oz) red cabbage, core removed and very finely grated

225g (7½oz) light soft brown sugar

175g (6oz) dried cranberries or dried berry and cherry mix

2 bay leaves

6 juniper berries, crushed

4 tablespoons balsamic vinegar

300ml (½ pint) red wine

salt and pepper

Heat the oil in a medium saucepan. Add the onions, cover with a lid and cook over a medium heat for 10 minutes until softened.

Add all the remaining ingredients, season with salt and pepper and bring to the boil. Then reduce the heat, re-cover and simmer for 30 minutes.

Uncover the pan and cook over a medium heat for a further 10 minutes or until the liquid has reduced to a syrupy consistency.

Serve warm or set to one side to cool before transferring to a sterilized Kilner or other preserving jar or a jam jar and sealing. This will keep for up to 1 week in the refrigerator.

Roast Tomato Chutney is superb squished on to olive oil toast or as a side for your brunch, picnic or barbecue. Meltingly soft, the Sweet Pepper Chutney (below) is wonderful as a topping for risottos, pulled through pasta or dolloped on a homemade burger.

Roast Tomato Chutney

MAKES ONE 225G (7½OZ) JAR OR SERVES 4

450g (14½oz) cherry tomatoes

3 tablespoons olive oil

2 tablespoons balsamic vinegar

2 tablespoons demerara sugar

2 dried chillies, roughly broken up

salt and pepper

Preheat the oven to 160°C/fan 150°C/325°F/Gas Mark 3.

Toss the tomatoes with all the remaining ingredients in a small roasting tin and season to taste with salt and pepper.

Bake for 1¾ hours until softened and split, but be careful not to allow the sugary juices to burn on the base of the tin – simply add a splash of water if too dry.

Allow to cool, then transfer to a sterilized Kilner or other preserving jar or a jam jar and seal. The chutney will keep for 3–4 days in the refrigerator.

Sweet Pepper Chutney

SERVES 4

3 tablespoons olive oil

2 large red peppers, cored, deseeded and finely sliced

2 large orange peppers, cored, deseeded and finely sliced

2 bay leaves

3 tablespoons caster sugar

2 garlic cloves, peeled but kept whole

½ small bunch of soft young thyme, snipped

salt and pepper

Heat the oil in a medium saucepan and stir in the peppers, bay leaves, sugar, garlic cloves and thyme. Place a piece of wet, crushed greaseproof paper over the pepper mixture and cover with a lid. Cook gently for 35–40 minutes or until the peppers are meltingly soft.

Remove the paper from the pan and increase the heat to reduce the liquid for about 3–4 minutes. Season to taste with salt and pepper.

Allow to cool, then transfer to a sterilized Kilner or other preserving jar or a jam jar and seal. The chutney will keep for 1 week in the refrigerator.

Why buy ready-made vinaigrette when you can make it this quickly? Delicious drizzled over a baked potato or spooned over veggies, or simply keep in the refrigerator and use to dress your salads. Serve the Warm Ginger & Orange Sesame Dressing (below) over noodles or spooned over hot rice. This dressing is also great with fresh tuna or strips of steak.

Honey, Mustard & Cider Vinaigrette

SERVES 6

2 tablespoons wholegrain mustard

3 tablespoons cider vinegar

8 tablespoons olive, rapeseed or sunflower oil

1 tablespoon clear honey

1–2 tablespoons water

salt and pepper

Place all the ingredients in a sterilized Kilner or other preserving jar or a jam jar. Season well with salt and pepper, seal and shake well.

Store in the refrigerator until needed. Bring to room temperature and shake again before using.

Warm Ginger & Orange Sesame Dressing

SERVES 4

2 tablespoons sesame seeds

2.5-cm (1-inch) piece of fresh root ginger, peeled and grated

1 large garlic clove, crushed

1 red chilli, deseeded and finely chopped

4 tablespoons sunflower oil

3 tablespoons dark soy sauce

juice of 2 oranges

2 teaspoons sesame oil

salt and pepper

Toast the sesame seeds in a small frying pan over a medium heat until golden.

Add the ginger, garlic and chilli and cook for 30 seconds. Stir in the remaining ingredients.

Season to taste with salt and pepper and serve warm. Alternatively, set to one side to cool before transferring to a sterilized Kilner or other preserving jar or a jam jar and sealing. This will keep for up to 1 week in the refrigerator.

This creamy tarragon dressing is great pulled through baby new potatoes, or use it as a delicious dip with chips or fish goujons. My favourite way to serve the Smoked Pepper Rouille (below) is spooned over a big fish stew or bowl of steamed mussels.

Soured Cream & Tarragon Dressing

SERVES 4

150ml (¼ pint) dairy-free single cream

2 teaspoons Dijon mustard

1 tablespoon chopped tarragon leaves

squeeze of lemon juice

salt and pepper

Place all the ingredients in a small bowl and gently mix together.

Season to taste with salt and pepper.

Smoked Pepper Rouille

SERVES 4–6

2 large red peppers

1 tablespoon olive oil

25g (1oz) crustless dairy-free white bread, soaked in a little water for 1 minute and excess water squeezed out

2 garlic cloves, crushed

1 teaspoon cayenne pepper

100ml (3½fl oz) extra virgin olive oil

salt and pepper

Preheat the oven to 210°C/fan 190°C/425°F/Gas Mark 7.

Place the peppers on a baking sheet, drizzle over the oil and roast for 35–40 minutes or until the peppers have slightly blackened, turning them occasionally.

Transfer the peppers to a large plastic food bag, seal and allow to cool.

Remove the peppers from the bag, reserving any of the juices. Peel off the skin, halve and remove the seeds.

Place the pepper flesh in a small food processor with the bread, garlic, cayenne and the pepper juices and whizz until smooth. With the blender or food processor running, slowly drizzle in the extra virgin olive oil. Season to taste with salt and pepper.

Classic Pesto, the taste of summer! Use both the stalks and the leaves of the basil for extra flavour. Walnuts, cashews and almonds can also be used in place of the traditional pine nuts. As for the Broad Bean & Basil Pistou (below), try serving it on toasted croutes topped with griddled mackerel fillets and a watercress and orange salad. If using fresh broad beans, you may have to skin them unless they are very, very young.

Classic Pesto

SERVES 4

1 small bunch of basil, stalks and leaves

1 large garlic clove, crushed

4 tablespoons pine nuts

150ml (¼ pint) olive oil

40g (1½oz) dairy-free strong Cheddar-style cheese, finely grated

salt and pepper

Wash the basil and add to a small food processor with the water still clinging to it – this will help lighten the pesto. Add the garlic, pine nuts and oil and whizz until thoroughly combined. Be careful not to over-blend – the mixture should be coarse, not smooth and gloopy.

Add the cheese to the food processor and whizz for a few seconds more. Season well with salt and pepper.

Broad Bean & Basil Pistou

SERVES 4–6

300g (10oz) frozen baby broad beans

4 tablespoons capers, drained

2 garlic cloves, crushed

3 anchovy fillets, drained and torn

1 large bunch of basil

250ml (8fl oz) extra virgin olive oil

salt and pepper

Place the broad beans in a saucepan, cover with boiling water and set aside for 2 minutes. Drain and rinse under cold water. Set aside to drain thoroughly.

Transfer the broad beans to a food processor with the capers, garlic, anchovies and basil. Pulse in 2-second bursts to form a coarse paste. Trickle in the oil quickly, while pulsing for a few bursts.

Season to taste with pepper and a little salt if needed. Cover and chill until needed. It will keep in the refrigerator for 2–3 days.

This creamy mayo has a subtle hint of smoked garlic and citrus, and will keep for days in the refrigerator. Don't be tempted to use all olive oil, otherwise it will taste too strong. The speedy, spicy Curry Gravy (below) is great with roasted salmon or pan-fried prawns, or serve it on the side with roast chicken as a zingy gravy alternative. Try it drizzled in a crusty baked sweet potato topped with juicy prawns.

Smoked Garlic & Chive Mayo

SERVES 4–6

2 egg yolks

1 teaspoon Dijon mustard

1 teaspoon smoked garlic salt, plus extra to taste if needed

300ml (½ pint) grapeseed oil or a mixture of extra virgin olive oil and grapeseed oil

squeeze of orange juice

2 tablespoons chopped chives

pepper

Place the egg yolks in a bowl with the mustard and smoked garlic salt and whisk together.

Gradually whisk in half the oil in a slow steady stream. When the mayonnaise starts to become very thick, add the orange juice. Gradually whisk in the remaining oil.

Season to taste with pepper, and extra garlic salt if needed, and stir through the chives.

Curry Gravy

SERVES 4

2 tablespoons Madras curry paste

1 tablespoons tomato purée

400ml (14fl oz) can coconut milk

squeeze of lemon juice

salt and pepper

Heat a medium saucepan, add the curry paste and tomato purée and fry for 30 seconds.

Add the coconut milk and simmer for 5 minutes. Finish with a squeeze of lemon juice and season to taste with salt and pepper.

You can't beat homemade chicken stock. You can prepare it as below by poaching a whole chicken or use leftovers from the Sunday roast chicken. Either way, it will be full of flavour.

A poached chicken may not look very exciting, but boy is it succulent, tasty and incredibly versatile – just pull away the cooled meat from the carcass, ready for dressing up. Add it to quick, stylish salads, scatter it over pizza or use it to make a great chicken pie. For a hearty chowder, simply replace the haddock in the recipe on page 52 with poached chicken pieces.

Citrus Chicken Stock Pot

MAKES ABOUT 2 LITRES (3½ PINTS)

1 free-range chicken, about 1.5kg (3lb)

1 onion, finely sliced

2 carrots, finely sliced

2 celery sticks, finely sliced

3 bay leaves

6 black peppercorns

a few thyme sprigs

2 thick unwaxed lemon slices

Remove the trussing string from the chicken and then pull away any loose fat from the rear end of the bird. Place in a large saucepan or stock pot.

Add all the remaining ingredients to the pan and barely cover with cold water.

Bring to the boil and skim off any fat or scum. Reduce the heat and simmer gently for about 1½ hours until the chicken is cooked through, making sure that the chicken remains submerged – you may have to weigh it down with a small plate. The legs should feel wobbly and loose when it's ready.

Remove the chicken from the stock and set to one side to cool. Strain the stock, skim off any fat and allow to cool. Cover and refrigerate until needed.

To store the stock in the freezer, boil the strained stock rapidly until reduced to about 400ml (14fl oz) so that it's very concentrated. Allow to cool, then pour into ice cube trays and freeze. You can then use the frozen cubes as you would a stock cube.

To get the maximum flavour from the root vegetables, make sure you finely slice them all. The addition of herbs and sun-dried tomato paste gives this stock real oomph.

Bouquet Garni Stock

MAKES ABOUT 1.2 LITRES (2 PINTS)

1 tablespoon olive oil

3 celery sticks, finely chopped

1 onion, finely sliced

2 large carrots, finely sliced

2 large thyme sprigs

3 bay leaves

handful of parsley stalks, bruised

2 tablespoons sun-dried tomato paste

20 black peppercorns

1.8 litres (3 pints) cold water

Heat the oil in a large saucepan, add the vegetables and herbs and cook over a medium heat for 10 minutes or until golden.

Stir in the tomato paste and cook for 3 minutes.

Add the peppercorns and measurement water and bring to the boil, then reduce the heat and simmer gently for 1 hour.

Allow to cool, then strain, cover and refrigerate until needed.

Index

Acknowledgements

Author's acknowledgements

Putting a book together is all about team work! Thank you to Stephanie Jackson at Octopus for giving me this opportunity and Alex Stetter, my editor, for all her hard work and patience. Thank you to Jaz Bahra, for the fab layouts and design, to Liz and Max Haarala Hamilton for all the stunningly beautiful photography and to Kat Mead for being such a talent in the kitchen.

Many thanks to my family, Tim, Isaac and Scouty, who chomped their way through this book and are my biggest critics! To Liz Raymont for patiently (and politely) checking and rechecking, always with a smile on her face.

Last but certainly not least, thank you to my sister, Jacks McDonnell Waters, who has always been so dedicated and a total talent to work with. As always, Jacks, such a great pleasure, and I dedicate this book to you, with much love.

About the author

Lesley Waters is a regular chef on *Ready Steady Cook*, *Great Food Live* and *This Morning*, but she is also the former head tutor of Leith's School of Food & Wine, a qualified fitness instructor and a mother of two. She likes to cook seasonal food whenever possible and her simple, modern style creates recipes that are easy to follow, with stunning results. Teaching has always been Lesley's great passion and opening her own cookery school on the Somerset/Dorset border is the realization of a long-held dream. Her energetic and quirky style of presentation is expertly combined with clear and simple guidance, making her classes both entertaining and informative. Details are available at www.lesleywaters.com

Dedicated to Jacks McDonnell-Waters

An Hachette UK Company
www.hachette.co.uk
First published in Great Britain in 2015
by Hamlyn, a division of
Octopus Publishing Group Ltd
Carmelite House
50 Victoria Embankment
London EC4Y 0DZ

www.octopusbooks.co.uk

First published as *Deliciously Dairy Free* in 2015
This paperback edition published in 2017

Copyright © Octopus Publishing Group Ltd 2015
Text copyright © Lesley Waters 2015

All rights reserved. No part of this work may be reproduced or utilized in any form or by any means, electronic or mechanical, including photocopying, recording or by any information storage and retrieval system, without the prior written permission of the publisher.

Lesley Waters asserts the moral right to be identified as the author of this work

ISBN 978 0 60063 454 6

A CIP catalogue record for this book is available from the British Library

Printed and bound in China

10 9 8 7 6 5 4 3 2 1

Publishing Director - Stephanie Jackson
Art Director - Jonathan Christie
Design - Jaz Bahra
Project Editor - Alex Stetter
Illustrations - Abigail Read
Photography - Haarala Hamilton
Home Economist - Kat Mead
Nutritionist - Angela Dowden
Production Controller - Sarah-Jayne Johnson